TWO HUNDRED AND NINETY-TWO ACTIVITIES FOR LITERATURE AND LANGUAGE ARTS

TNT

TWO HUNDRED
AND NINETY-
TWO
ACTIVITIES FOR
LITERATURE
AND LANGUAGE
ARTS

Eve Geiger

Fearon Teacher Aids
Simon & Schuster Supplementary Education Group

To Larry
Without his help and encouragement, this book
would never have become a reality

Illustrator: Tracy Hall

ISBN 0-8224-6746-1
Printed in the United States of America
1. 9 8 7 6 5 4 3 2

CONTENTS

Future...84. A Press Conference...85. Prose into
Poetry...86. Puppetry...87. A Radio Script...88. Rebus
Stories...89. A Roller Movie...90. Scene Locations...
91. Sequels...92. Solution Letters...93. A Story Frieze...
94. Story Illustrations...95. Story Mapping...96. Story
Panels...97. Story Update...98. A Student Book
Jacket...99. Taped Review...100. Telegram Reports...
101. Then and Now/There and Here...102. This Is Your
Life...103. Three-dimensional Picture Map...104. The
Three W's...105. A Time Line...106. Twenty
Questions...107. TV Anchor Report...108. Wide
Reading...109. Write It as a Poem...110. "Why"
Stories...111. You Are There

      128.–139. Folk Stories
      140.–147. Modern Fantasy
      148.–157. Animals That Talk
      158.–167. Famous People (Biographies)
      168.–177. Survival
      178.–186. Children of Other Cultures
        and Countries
      187.–195. Monsters, Dragons, and Such
      196.–206. People Who Write Books
      207.–220. Sports
      221.–230. Medieval Adventure Stories
      231.–240. Greek Mythology
      241.–247. Families
      248.–256. Friendship
      257.–264. Mysteries
      265.–274. Historical Fiction
      275.–283. Loneliness
      284.–292. Animals

INTRODUCTION

This book has been designed to provide a wide variety of activities that can be used with any literature book. Skills related to comprehension, sequencing, plot development, vocabulary growth, character analysis, and creative writing are inherent in almost every activity. It is beyond the scope of this book, however, to deal with all the deeper feelings and meanings that are an integral part of any effective literature program; that is up to you, the teacher.

The ideas presented here are the result of my work with creative teachers, librarians, students, authors, and colleagues at the elementary, secondary, and university levels—and of my affinity for collecting ideas from every available source over the years. My interest has always been to discover successful and stimulating methods of teaching. The ideas suggested are not all new and original, but it seems to me that it is helpful to have them all under one cover.

This book is divided into several sections, beginning with general activities that can be used with any books the students have read or have had read to them. These activities will help them enjoy literature while sharpening their reading, writing, speaking, and listening skills. Following the title of each activity is a key noting the type of activity and for whom it is designed. Following the description of the activity is the specific skill or skills it emphasizes.

The second section offers some activities that can nurture students' understanding and enjoyment of poetry.

Theme teaching is described in the third part of the book, which includes examples of themes and some suggested activities and book lists for each theme.

The final sections are additional aids: questions to stimulate book discussions, suggestions for successful group work, and an extensive professional bibliography. I have found Charlotte Huck's *Literature in the Elementary School* a particularly valuable resource in my teaching and writing and strongly recommend it as a reference to anyone teaching literature. It is almost as valuable as frequent conferences with a children's librarian.

I have not attempted to categorize the activities or book lists by grade level, since the ability range of any group is wide. You can easily adapt the ideas, however, to meet the needs of your class.

Throughout the book I emphasize the importance of preparation, presentation, and follow-up for both teacher and student, since these are the major components of any effective lesson.

I hope that these activities will not only teach but also be enjoyed by all participants and that students will be motivated to become true readers of literature beyond the classroom.

GENERAL ACTIVITIES

After the name of each activity is a key describing who it's for—an individual student (I), a group of students (G), a parent-student project (P-S), or a classroom exhibit (CE)—and what kind of activity it is—writing, reading, listening, discussion, art, speaking, dramatic expression, research. After the description of each activity is a list of the skills it strengthens—such as fluency, vocabulary building, comprehension, character analysis, plot analysis, creative writing, and critical thinking.

1

Alike and Different (I, G; reading, discussion)
Students make two lists, one of characters that are alike in various books and one of characters that are different. Each set of characters should have a notation as to how they are alike or different. Each student then reads the list aloud for discussion of the choices and the reasons for the choices.
(Skills: character analysis, critical thinking)

2

An Alphabet Story (I; writing)
Students write an alphabet story listing characters and elements in the story. For example,
   A is for armor worn by the knights.
   B is for Butts at which arrows were shot.
   C is for Camelot, King Arthur's home.
(Skill: vocabulary building)

3

Anonymous Autobiographies (I; writing, speaking)
Each student writes an autobiography of a favorite character, and then reads it to the class to see if the character can be identified. In order to do this well, the "author" must be familiar with the character and events in his or her life.
(Skills: comprehension, character analysis)

4

Another Ending (I; art)
Children who have difficulty with spelling and writing draw a picture of what might have happened if the story had had a different ending. Other children may enjoy drawing a picture to accompany their written new ending.
(Skills: comprehension, plot analysis)

Author of the Month (CE; research, writing, listening)

5

Select an author to highlight each month. Gather book covers, posters, articles, and other material for a bulletin board display. Display books by the author. Select one or more of the books to read aloud, depending on their difficulty and length (for example, several books by Beatrix Potter but only one or two by Laura Ingalls Wilder or one by Lloyd Alexander).

Tell or read the story of the author's life to small children. Older students can research the author's life on their own and share their findings. Students can create stories similar to the author's. Many fine cassettes and filmstrips related to authors are available from audiovisual departments. (For other ideas about teaching about authors, see activities 196–206.)
(Skills: critical thinking, creative writing)

An Author's Point of View (G; reading, discussion)

6

Several students who have read the same story discuss how the author's point of view is incorporated in the story. They'll need to review what the characters do and say and how the plot develops. Such a discussion involves comprehension at the highest level, taking the reader beyond the literal words of the story.
(Skills: comprehension, plot analysis, character analysis)

Autobiographies (I; reading, writing)

7

Each student writes an autobiography of a person, an animal, or an object related to a story or theme. They might write autobiographies about pennies, hats, miners, or llamas. Because this activity requires the student to look at events in the story through the eyes of the selected character or object, it offers an opportunity for creative thinking.
(Skills: comprehension, plot analysis, character analysis)

Book Clubs (G; reading, listening, discussion)

8

Capitalize on small childrens' enjoyment in reading to each other. Divide the class into pairs for a "reading club" period. Let the pairs select any place in the room (a corner, a closet, under your desk) to take

turns reading a story or a portion of a story to one another. Follow this session by a sharing period to allow them to discuss and critique what they have read.
(Skills: fluency, comprehension, critical thinking)

Book Comparisons (G; reading, discussion)
Students who have read the same thematically related books discuss the characters' likenesses and differences. (Examples of thematically related books are *Island of the Blue Dolphins, My Side of the Mountain,* and *Call It Courage* about survival, or *Caddie Woodlawn, Pippi Longstocking, Little House on the Prairie,* and *The Good Master* about a girl's trials and tribulations in a particular environment.) To stimulate the discussion, pose such questions as, If the characters in the various books swapped environments, would they still behave the same? Could the characters exchange places? How would the other characters in the book react to such a change?
(Skills: comprehension, character analysis)

Book Map (G, CE; reading, discussion)
On a world map, pin a tag with the title of each book the children have read on the country in which it is set. This geographical lesson can stimulate discussions about similarities and differences in the ways characters dress and behave. Students will also be interested to see that versions of the same folk story or fairy tale appear in several different countries (such as *Cinderella* or *The Three Wishes*).
(Skills: character analysis, critical thinking)

Bookmarks (I; art)
Each student illustrates a bookmark with "the part I liked best" or "my favorite character." Encourage creativity in shape, size, media, and illustration; don't allow copying a picture or design from the book.
(Skill: comprehension)

Book Review (I, CE; reading, discussion, writing)
Students pretend they are book reviewers for the local newspaper. To prepare, have them bring in book reviews from newspapers and magazines they find at home or in

the school library. (Be sure to warn the librarian of the impending onslaught.) Then have the students spend considerable time reading and discussing these reviews. They should focus on their objectivity and on their treatment of both the positive and negative points of the book.

Now each student is ready to write a review of a recently read book. After the reviews are completed, allow time for reading the reviews aloud and discussing them.

Ask the librarian if the reviews could be displayed in the library for the benefit of the whole school. If this is not feasible, set aside a bulletin board in the room for an ongoing display.
(Skills: comprehension, critical thinking)

13
Bury a Book (I or G; reading, discussion)
Students select a book to be buried in a time capsule. Rationale for the book chosen must be explicit and complete.

If this is a group project, it will engender much discussion of the reasons why a certain book should be chosen for such an important purpose.
(Skill: critical thinking)

14
Cartoon Collections (I or G, P-S; research)
Students make individual scrapbooks or contribute to a bulletin board of cartoons containing allusions to literature. When the scrapbooks or bulletin board are finished, have the students explain their choices. This project creatively demonstrates how literature pervades our everyday life.
(Skill: critical thinking)

15
Change the Action (I; reading, writing, discussion)
From a favorite book, each student selects a paragraph that describes much action and then changes the verbs to give the paragraph an entirely different meaning. Students can share their rewritten paragraphs aloud and discuss the power of words.
(Skills: vocabulary building, comprehension)

16
Change the Setting (I; reading, writing, discussion)
Each student rewrites a story, changing the setting to a different place or time. Students can share their stories aloud and discuss the power of words.
(Skills: comprehension, creative writing)

17

Change the Description (I; reading, writing, discussion)
From a book the student or the class has read, each student selects a paragraph that has particularly descriptive language and then rewrites it, using synonyms—or antonyms—for the descriptive words and phrases. Students can share their rewritten paragraphs aloud and discuss how changing words changes shading and nuance. Prompt the discussion with such questions as, Do we get the same picture from the new paragraph that we did from the author's original version? Why do you think the author chose the particular words used in the story? How important is the choice of words in writing a story? Students should use examples from the stories to prove their points.
(Skills: comprehension, creative writing, critical thinking)

18

Character-Book Match (I; reading)
Make two sets of cards, one with the names of characters in books read by the students and the other with the names of the books. The player shuffles the two decks and matches the cards. You can also add a third set with the names of authors of the books. This is an effective activity for a literature center.
(Skill: comprehension)

19

Character Change (I; reading, writing)
To aid their understanding of a character, students write two descriptions of a chosen character: one at the beginning of the story and another at the end of the story. They should note how the character has changed and what he or she has learned.
(Skills: character analysis, comprehension)

20

Character Conversations (G; speaking, dramatic expression)
Students assume the roles of various fictional characters and carry on conversations with each other. This exercise entails an understanding of the character and a knowledge of the times and places mentioned in the story. You might have classmates listen to the conversations and critique them for accuracy.
(Skills: character analysis, comprehension)

21

Character Dolls (I; art, writing)
Students dress dolls to depict various characters in a story. The dolls can be made of papier-mâché, clay, rags, or cut paper.

After students have made their dolls, they might write an autobiography for each doll.
(Skills: reading for detail, comprehension, character analysis)

Character Interviews (G; speaking, reading, research)
Select one student to be an interviewer and select other students to be book characters. The interviewer will, of course, have to have read the books from which the characters have been chosen in order to prepare the questions to be asked (although other class members may help out). Remind students that TV and radio interviewers prepare themselves in the same way, that is, by becoming familiar with their interviewees. Following the interview, you might invite questions from the audience. Several sets of interviews may be prepared at the same time.
(Skills: plot and character comprehension)

22

Character Traits (I; reading)
To study how an author develops a character, students each select a trait in a particular character and review the story to see how the author has revealed it—by simply stating it, by things the character does or says, or by things someone else in the story does or says.
(Skills: character analysis, critical thinking)

23

A Character Visit (I; reading, speaking or writing)

An imaginary visit from a story character provides an opportunity for students to think about such questions as, How would the character act? What could we do to make him or her feel comfortable? Would our society seem strange? Have each student describe the visit of a chosen character in writing or orally (oral presentations are more fun). To describe a character's visit, the student must know the story and the character well.
(Skills: comprehension, character analysis)

24

25

A Class Mural (I or G; art)
Individuals or small groups who have read the same book make a mural of scenes from the book. For each book, mount a large piece of butcher paper on a wall or chalkboard. Divide the paper into interesting shapes for each scene to be represented. Chalk and tempera paint produce the most colorful murals. Cut paper can also be pasted on the background to represent tree trunks, leaves, or palm fronds.

Before starting on the mural itself, each group should decide which scenes they will include, who will do which scene, and which shape each scene will go in. They should then do a preliminary sketch of the mural. This preparation allows the painters an opportunity to discuss and decide what should be depicted, who should do what to accomplish it, and what media should be used. Both individual and group murals have the advantage, if they are well organized, of answering the eternal question, What do we do when we finish . . . our math . . . our workbook? (Skills: comprehension, critical thinking)

26

The Climax (G; reading, discussion)
To develop recognition of story structure, ask the children to find the climax of the story they are reading and then to list the ways the author built up to it.
(Skills: comprehension, sequencing, plot analysis)

27

Collages (I; art)
Each student makes a collage about a selected story. Students can draw the pictures for their collages or cut them out of old magazines. The pictures should be mounted collage-style on 12-by-18-inch construction paper. When the collages are done, have each student explain his or hers, including the reasons

for selecting each picture. Because this activity requires much rereading to get ideas for appropriate pictures, it encourages students to read for detail.
(Skills: comprehension, sequencing)

Combine the Characters (I; writing)
Ask the students to imagine what would happen if several

28 characters from different stories got together. Then have them each write a story describing that meeting. To write an effective story, the students must understand how each character talks, acts, and thinks. Students might share their stories aloud and then contrast the various treatments of the same characters.

Individually or in groups, students could also write a play describing the meeting of the characters. Have students read their plays aloud or perform them.
(Skills: comprehension, character analysis)

Comic Strips (I; reading, art)
Students make a comic strip of a chosen episode in a story. They first fold or divide a 6-by-12-inch strip of paper into four or five sections. Then they draw cartoon-style pictures (and dialogue written in balloons) showing the sequence of

29 events in the episode. The cartoons may be line drawings or colored in, but all the cartoonists should be sure to title their work and to sign it! Some students may wish to make a series of cartoons, like the Prince Valiant comic strip.
(Skills: sequencing, comprehension, character analysis)

Comparisons (I or G; writing or discussion)
"This story reminds me of _____" can lead your students into an exercise comparing how a problem is solved in different ways in two (or more) books. Use a two-column

30 list with the headings "Likenesses" and "Differences" to briefly make the comparisons. Students can develop their own lists, or you can record the results of a class discussion on the blackboard.
(Skills: comprehension, critical thinking)

Construct a Diorama (I or G, P-S; reading, art)
Each student or group of students makes a diorama of a scene in a chosen story. (Your class may be interested to learn that dioramas are sometimes used in the making of movies and television programs to determine how the scenery and placement of characters will blend.)

31
Construct dioramas in cut-down cartons, using such materials as papier-mâché, clay, sand, wood, and miniature toys. A variation is a miniature stage complete with back-drop, curtain, and stand-up figures made from construction paper with cardboard back supports.

This is an effective child-parent activity that will require rereading the story and working out the plans together. (For students who do not have a parent to help them, find a friend, an older student, or school aide or volunteer to substitute.) Dioramas make effective displays for parent's night or other special programs for parents.
(Skills: comprehension, visual imaging)

Create a Scene (I; writing or discussion)
To answer the question, What might have happened in between? students write a scene that might have happened before or after a selected one in a book. To find the places
32 for potential new scenes, look for cues to jumps in time such as "the next day," "two weeks later," or "later in the day."
(Skills: comprehension, character analysis, plot analysis, creative writing)

Creative Writing Cards (I; writing)
Prepare three sets of cards in the categories of person, place, and thing. On each card put a word or phrase from a book that has just been read aloud (or that all the students
33 have read) or from a particular theme or topic. For example, if you've just read a book about life in the Middle Ages, you might have "person cards" for the words *princess* and *peasant,* "place cards" for *castle* and *cave,* and "thing

cards" for *ball of yarn* and *gold piece*. (You can have several cards with the same word so that you don't have to run out of familiar words or concepts.) Each student then draws a card from each category and uses the three cards as the basis for an original story. This activity can be adapted for any genre—science fiction, mystery, biography, sports.
(Skill: creative writing)

Crossword Puzzle (I or G; reading, writing)

34

¹A	N	I	²M	³A	L	⁴S
R						N
T		⁵A	N	T		A
⁶I		⁷				K
C	A	T		⁸		E

Each student or a group of students creates a crossword puzzle using the people, events, things, and places in a particular story. The rest of the class solves the puzzle.
(Skill: comprehension)

Decorated Book Jackets (I; reading, art)
Each student designs and decorates a book jacket of a chosen story. The book jacket should include a synopsis of the story and a biographical sketch of the author. This project requires the student to recognize the main idea or turning point of the plot.
(Skills: comprehension, critical thinking)

35

Descriptive Paragraphs (I; reading, art)
A student can make an attractive booklet by copying and illustrating (with crayons or watercolors) particularly descriptive paragraphs from books that he or she has read. If two or more students have selected the same paragraph, a comparison of their visualizations of it can stimulate a thoughtful discussion.
(Skills: comprehension, visual imaging)

36

Dialogue Extension (G; reading, discussion)
Select several scenes that have a minimum of dialogue. Divide the class into several groups, and appoint a scribe for each group. Assign one of the scenes to each group with directions to extend the dialogue by answering the question, What else do you think they could have said? After each group reads its dialogue aloud, have the class discuss how accurately the dialogue fits the characters. (Your students may be interested to learn that this is a

37

technique used by scriptwriters to adapt a novel for television or the movies.)
(Skills: comprehension, character analysis)

Diaries and Logs (I; writing)

38

Each student creates a diary or log of a favorite character. The diary may be based on events in the book, or it may be based on invented events that could have happened during or after the original story. Encourage students to be the character whose diary they are writing. Plan a special time for students to share their diaries.
(Skills: comprehension, character analysis)

Different Action (I; writing, discussion)

39 Each student writes a description of how they might have responded to a particular situation differently than the character did. If several students write about the same situation, the comparison of their descriptions can lead to a stimulating discussion about motivation and consequences.
(Skills: comprehension, character analysis)

Dramatizations (G; dramatic expression)
Dramatization offers students who have difficulty with written expression an opportunity to express themselves orally. With the students, divide a story into scenes. Decide what characters will be needed, discuss them, and assign the parts. Having several casts will allow for wider partici-

40 pation and for discussion of role interpretation (stress that there is no one "correct" interpretation).

Students may write their parts or ad lib them, and the properties, scenery, and costumes can be imaginary or fairly realistic. But to keep the focus on oral expression, keep the production simple.
(Skills: comprehension, creative expression, character analysis)

A Fan-fold Book (I; art)
Each student makes a fan-fold book to show the sequence

41 of events in a story. Cut a large piece of paper into long strips that are 8–10 inches wide, or tape together single pieces of paper. The strip is folded accordion style, and the

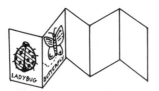

student colors or draws scenes from the story in sequence on the sections. The final step is a one-line explanation printed at the bottom of each picture to enable the viewer to follow the story.

(Skills: sequencing, plot analysis)

Father and Mother Roles (G; discussion, speaking)

42 A panel of students discusses the roles of father and mother as depicted in books read by the group. (For more ideas about teaching stories about families, see activities 241–247.)

(Skills: comprehension, critical thinking)

Feltboard Stories (I; speaking)

Feltboard characters are an excellent vehicle for story-telling, particularly in the primary grades. Have your students use the feltboard characters to retell the story in their own words.

43 Draw and color characters and objects from a story on paper, Velcro, or felt (paper is the least expensive and works just as well as the other materials). You might also paint a variety of background scenes (country, city, farm, river, ocean) on large pieces of flannelette.

Older students may enjoy preparing a feltboard story to tell to younger children.

(Skills: sequencing, comprehension)

File Box Reviews (I; writing)

Class members contribute to a file box of thumbnail book reviews. Divide a small file box into genres such as mystery, science fiction, biographies, and animal stories. When a student finishes a book, he or she files a 3-by-5-inch card

44 with the book's title, author, several sentences describing the story (enough to arouse interest, but not enough to spoil the story for a prospective reader), and a brief evaluation. If the evaluation is negative, an explanation should be provided.

(Skills: comprehension, critical thinking)

Flashbacks (I; writing)

45 Students may try writing a familiar story as a flashback, beginning with an event that happened toward the end of

the story. Discuss the technique and how it is used in television and the movies.
(Skills: comprehension, plot analysis)

Folklore and Fantasy Characters (I and G; various)

A class collection of fairy-tale and folk-story characters—such as animals, princesses, kings, queens, dwarfs, and trolls—can motivate many creative activities. Have your students bring in (or make) dolls, stuffed animals, toys, miniatures, cut-outs, and other representations of fantasy characters, and make a display of them. (You'll be amazed at what the collection call will bring forth!)

46

Have the students select three of the characters and compose a story about them. They can tell the story aloud or write it or turn it into a play. They can also create a conversation between two of the characters. These props are also useful for retelling a story. (For more ideas about teaching folk and fantasy stories, see activities 128–139 and 187–195.)
(Skills: fluency, creative writing)

A Glossary of Terms (G; reading)

47

Students contribute to a glossary of terms related to a selected literary theme. Start the glossary on a large piece of tagboard and keep a felt pen nearby. As students discover new words and phrases in their reading, they add them to the glossary. To encourage participation, each entry should include the student's initials and his or her explanation of the meaning of the word or phrase.
(Skill: vocabulary building)

Guess Who (G; reading, discussion)

48

Children of all ages enjoy guessing games. After a number of students have read the same books or stories, they can prepare a series of clues for a Guess Who game. The clues

should range from easy to difficult and should be peculiar to the particular character or setting. Developing good clues requires rereading for detail.
(Skill: comprehension)

Guest Author (G; listening, discussion)
Invite an author to discuss his or her books and to describe the process of publishing a book. Authors of children's and young people's books usually welcome such an opportunity to get feedback from their readers.

49   Prepare for the visit with wide reading and discussion of the author's books. To ensure that the visit is a satisfactory learning experience, the class should also prepare a list of questions they would like to ask and a list of topics they would like to hear the author discuss. Of course, the preparation should also include a display of the author's books and any original stories by the students.
(Skills: comprehension, critical thinking)

Headlines (I; writing)
Budding journalists enjoy writing headlines about an event in a book they have read. This is a challenging exercise because it requires conveying the essence of an event in just

50   a few words. For example, "Children Spend the Night in a Museum" might be written about the children in *From the Mixed Up Files of Mrs. Basil E. Frankweiler,* or "Rats Escape from Government Laboratory, Scientists Fear Results" might be the headline for *Mrs. Frisby and the Rats of NIMH.* Display the headlines on a bulletin board or place them in a box to use for a guessing game.
(Skills: vocabulary building, comprehension)

Illustrator of the Month (G; reading, discussion, art)
Select an illustrator to study each month. Display books and other examples of his or her work—as well

51   as the illustrator's picture—in the front of the room. (Because this is where students are often looking, they consciously or unconsciously absorb the material displayed there.)

Read stories illustrated or written by this artist and discuss the relationship of the pictures to the story. What media was used? Why was this particular media selected? Have students illustrate an original story using the media discussed.

Read about the illustrator's life. How did it affect the illustrations? Listen to tapes or watch videos about the illustrator, if any are available.
(Skills: visual imaging, critical thinking)

Interview an "Author" (I; speaking, reading, research)
Hold interviews with "authors" to discuss their books. Pairs of students become interviewer and author to discuss a book they both have read. The interviewer should prepare questions beforehand, and the audience may ask their own questions at the end of the interview. Because this activity requires familiarity not only with the book but with the author as well, students need to do some research about the author and look especially for insights into how the author's life influenced the story.
(Skills: fluency, comprehension, critical thinking)

52

Learning Centers (CE; various)
Organize an independent learning center with a variety of activities related to the current theme or to literature in general. Materials in the center might include an envelope of story starters, pockets containing who, what, and where statements for creative writing, a game of authors (which might be created by the students), materials for illustrating stories, and interesting skills sheets. To keep the center alive and effective, change the activities often.
(Skills: depend on the materials in learning center)

53

Letter Exchange (I; writing)
Here's a novel way to improve letter writing skills. Each student writes a letter to a book character. Then two students who have read the same book exchange letters and, assuming the role of the character, answer the other's letter.
(Skills: comprehension, critical thinking)

54

55

Life-size Figures (I; art, writing)
Each student draws a life-size figure of a favorite character on butcher paper and writes a short biography without disclosing the character's name. The other students try to identify the character. Primary graders usually prefer to draw familiar animal characters—Paddington, Curious George, or Frances. Older students may select Homer Price, Jim Davis, Laura Ingalls, or Henry Reed.

Use the figures as a display for a book exhibit.
(Skills: comprehension, critical thinking)

List the Details (G; discussion)
In order to facilitate participation in future activities related to a book or story, it is helpful to list the details an author has given about the character or characters and about the setting of the story, such as the house where somebody lived, the room the story happened in, or the

56 cave in the woods. If the book is one the whole class has read, the teacher can write the list on the chalkboard while the items evolve from class discussion. Or if a small group of students has read the same book, the group members can work together to create the list. Such lists can be kept close at hand for dramatizations, interviews, dioramas, murals, and other projects.
(Skills: reading for details)

Literary Football (G; writing, reading)
When a group has read several books, they can prepare questions about the stories to use in a game of Literary Football. Have the group discuss what makes a good question before they start formulating theirs.

To play Literary Football, start with a diagram of a
57 football field, including yardage lines, drawn on the chalkboard. Two teams take turns drawing questions. Yardage may be assigned to each question based on its difficulty, or each question may be worth five yards. A missed question means lost yardage. The team with the most touchdowns is the winner.
(Skills: comprehension, critical thinking)

The Little People (I; writing, research)

After reading stories of fantasy, have the class develop a collection of "little people" (elves, dwarfs, trolls, and so on). The students can bring toy figures from home or draw them or construct them from clay or papier-mâché. Each student can research the background of a selected "little person"—his or her characteristics and relation to the people in his or her native country. The results of this research can be as simple as a folk tale or as complex as a sociological treatise. (For more ideas about teaching folk and fantasy stories, see activities 128–139 and 187–195.) (Skills: critical thinking, character analysis)

58

Living Pictures (G; dramatic expression)
A group of students who have read the same book portray a few scenes as narrated tableaux vivants, or living scenes. This activity requires careful planning of which scenes to present, what kind of background and props to use, who will portray the characters, and how much narration to add.

59

To frame the tableaus, construct a large frame resembling a book with a cover that can open and close as each scene is changed.
(Skills: comprehension, visual imaging, creative thinking)

Lost and Found (I; writing)

Writing a lost-and-found advertisement for an object in a story is a simple activity that requires rereading for details. (Skill: comprehension)

60

A Magazine (I, G; writing, reading, art)
Students put together a magazine with illustrated columns, articles, and short stories "written" by characters and with book-based advertisements. Such a magazine's contents might include "Contrary Mary's Garden Column," an article by Karana *(Island of the Blue Dolphins)* on "First Impressions of Santa Barbara," and an advertisement for handmade puppets by the Geppetto Studio *(The*

61

Adventures of Pinocchio). The finished product may be assembled with a catchy name and an attractive cover. (Skills: creative writing, comprehension)

Main Ideas (G; discussion)

62 After you have finished a read-aloud book or a group has finished reading the same book, ask everyone to describe the main idea of the story. List all the comments on the chalkboard. Discuss the validity of each description. See if a consensus can be reached.
(Skills: comprehension, critical thinking)

A Memory Book (I; reading, writing)

63 Students make a book with an attractive cover. During the year, they use it to enter favorite poems, thoughts, and picturesque language and quotations they particularly like in books they read. They can keep original poems and other writing in the memory book as well.
(Skills: creative writing and expression)

Mental Imagery (G; listening)

64 To stimulate mental imagery, play tapes of Newbery or Caldecott Award winners and other good children's books. It is important that students read the book before listening to the tape, however, because familiarity with the story will enhance their appreciation of the imagery—and they will not be tempted to skip reading the book.
(Skill: visual imaging)

Miming a Story (G; dramatic expression)
Have one child read a story aloud while a selected cast mimes the action. This activity can be repeated with several different casts. One variation is to have the reader read the narrative parts only, while the cast improvises the dialogue.

65 After the performance, have the class discuss not only the acting merits but also the accuracy of the cast's story interpretation and character analysis.

Another variation is to have one group of students pantomime scenes from a story, while the rest of the class tries to guess the title. This makes an interesting activity to perform before another class that has read the same stories.
(Skills: comprehension, critical thinking)

Mobiles (I; art)

66 Students construct mobiles depicting characters or objects in a story. The items for the mobile can be cut out of paper, or they can be real miniatures. This activity will require much rereading and reading for detail. When the mobiles are completed, students explain their choice of objects to their classmates.
(Skill: comprehension)

More Details (I; writing)
Sometimes an author will merely mention that an event has occurred rather than describe it in detail. Students then have the opportunity to write about the **67** event in detail, drawing on their knowledge of the characters, the plot development, and the style of the author's writing.
(Skills: comprehension, creative writing)

New Characters (I or G; writing)
Students rewrite a story or a scene by changing the leading character— from boy to girl, elf to giant, fairy to witch, or **68** farmer to lawyer, for example. This can be an effective group activity with several children who have read the same

book. Discuss how the story is changed when a character is changed.
(Skills: comprehension, vocabulary building)

New Titles (G; writing)
After several students have read the same book, they discuss possible alternative titles. Because the title must **69** come from the story and have a special meaning, this discussion can help students understand the meaning of the story.
(Skills: comprehension, vocabulary building)

Newspaper Report (I; writing)

70 Students each select an event in a story and write it up as a newspaper article. Remind them that news items usually include who, what, when, where, and why. This activity strengthens the ability to isolate main ideas and important facts.
(Skills: comprehension, critical thinking)

One More Chapter (I; writing)

71 Students each write one more chapter for a selected book. This activity will require a thorough knowledge and understanding of the book.
(Skills: comprehension, vocabulary building)

Oral Book Reports (I; speaking)

72

To aid students in reviewing a book, have them think about the story in three parts—the introduction, the development of the plot, and the ending—to get the sequence clearly in mind. Sometimes it is helpful to have them answer the question, What is this story about? Emphasize that only main events—and few, if any details—should be used to answer the question. This exercise can help students find the main idea, which is often one of the most difficult skills to learn.
(Skills: comprehension, critical thinking)

Original Monsters (I; art, writing)

73 After students have read a number of folk stories, lead them in a discussion of the role of monsters (such as giants, ogres, dragons, and other beasts). Then have students create their own monsters out of papier-mâché, cut-paper sculpture, clay, paper bags—or simply drawn or painted on

large paper. Each monster should be given a name with special meaning, and its distinctive characteristics should be described in writing. The students may also write stories in which their monsters are the leading characters. (For more ideas about teaching books about monsters, see activities 187–195.)
(Skills: comprehension, creative writing and expression)

Our Book Friends (I, CE; art, writing)

74

An interesting variation on book reviews is to have students make drawings, cut-outs, or paper dolls of favorite characters in each book they read. They should label the drawings, briefly explain each character, and write a short review of the book. Add the characters and reviews to an ongoing bulletin board display. This display makes an interesting way for other students to learn about books they might want to read.
(Skills: comprehension, critical thinking)

Pairs of Characters (I; art)

75

This is a stimulating activity for students who are reading books set in other times and places. They can make two drawings (or cut-paper figures) of a selected character: one drawing shows how the character looks in the story, and the other drawing shows how that character would look today where you live. Be sure that the pictures are not copied, because one of the objectives of this activity is to stimulate mental imagery.
(Skills: comprehension, critical thinking, visual imaging)

Photographing the Story (I; writing)

76

Ask students to imagine they are photographers assigned to take three or four pictures of the key points in a particular story. Have them write descriptions of the pictures they would take. This task requires students to think through the

story, to determine the most important episodes, and to note the details in those episodes.
(Skills: comprehension, critical thinking, visual imaging)

77

A Picto-map (I or G; reading, art)
Each student or group of students draws a map of the locale of a selected story and places or draws pictures of characters, objects, or events at the appropriate locations. Picto-maps are especially effective for stories with action in many different places, such as *Wind in the Willows, Adam of the Road, My Side of the Mountain,* and various fairy tales and folk stories. This activity requires students to read for detail and to determine the key events of the story.
(Skills: comprehension, sequencing, critical thinking)

78

A Picture Diary (I; art)
A picture diary begins with a large sheet of construction paper divided into four sections and a title such as "A Day in the Life of _____," "A Week in the Life of _____," "A Difficult Period in the Life of _____," or "A Terrifying Time in the Life of _____." In each section the student draws one of a sequence of events from a selected story that illustrates the title of the picture diary.
(Skills: comprehension, critical thinking, visual imaging)

79

Picture-Phrase Match (I, G; reading, art)
Each student creates a picture of a book character to match a phrase or sentence from the book that describes the illustration. The pictures and quotations can be put in two boxes or envelopes and used as a game with a small group. The leader holds up a picture and the players in turn try to select the matching phrase or sentence.
(Skill: comprehension)

80

Picture Titles (G; reading, art)
Students draw titles in picture form (rebus). Their classmates then try to guess each title.
(Skill: comprehension)

81

Plot Development (I, G; reading, discussion)
A diagram is an excellent device for helping to understand plot development. One of two patterns may be used to record various events.

(climax)

— — — — —

— — — — —   — — — — —

— — — — — —   — — — — — —

— — — — (beginning)   (end)— — — — —

or

(beginning) — — — —   — — — —   — — — — (end)

Demonstrate book diagramming on the board after discussion of a book (or several books) familiar to the class. Then, throughout the year students can make a diagram of each book they read to use as a reference for discussions and other activities.
(Skills: comprehension, sequencing)

Poster Ads (I; art)
82
Following a discussion and some study of what makes an effective poster, each student creates a poster to "sell" a selected book. The posters should be large and colorful, and the picture or design should make the audience want to read the book. Students will need to consider not only the main ideas of the book but also what aspects of the book would make people want to "buy" it.
(Skills: comprehension, critical thinking)

Predictions of the Future (I; reading)

83
To increase understanding of plot development techniques, each student makes a list of foreshadowings, or hints to the reader about what is going to happen—such as "Little did he realize his plans could go awry" or "She did not realize then that her dream would never come true." The list can be made by reviewing the book or while reading it for the first time.
(Skills: comprehension, plot analysis, critical thinking)

A Press Conference (I and G; research, speaking)
84
Hold a press conference for an "author" or a book character. All participants will need to do independent research about the author's or character's life. Reporters should

prepare questions, and the "author" or "character" will need to be very well prepared in order to answer them. Have an "agent" or "manager" clearly state the ground rules for the conference (such as one question at a time and do not ask a question that has already been answered). The result can be an insightful and thought-provoking way to clarify a story and to have an in-depth discussion of it. (Skills: comprehension, critical thinking)

Prose into Poetry (I or G, CE; writing)
Following the study of narrative poems, have each student or group of students retell a favorite story in the form of a narrative poem. The results may be posted on a bulletin board or shared with another class. (For more ideas about teaching poetry, see activities 112–127.)
(Skills: comprehension, creative writing)

85

Puppetry (I; art, dramatic expression)

Puppets provide an enjoyable way to study character, and for shy youngsters, they make public speaking easier. Puppets can be made from papier-mâché, paper bags, or paper cut-outs attached to sticks. A large cardboard box or a small table turned on end can be a simple stage to hide the performers so that only the puppets are visible. Students may write the dialogue for the puppets, or they may use the dialogue from the story. Spontaneous dialogue is always fun, too. Enacting a scene from a book or story will require a thorough understanding of plot and characters.
(Skills: comprehension, critical thinking, creative writing)

86

A Radio Script (I or G; writing, dramatic expression)
Each student or group of students turns a scene or scenes from a story into a radio script. After the scenes to be dramatized are selected, dialogue and narrative must be created and sound effects and music must be specified. After your students write their scripts, let them enact the stories.
(Skills: comprehension, character analysis, critical thinking, creative writing)

87

Rebus Stories (I, writing, art)

Katy's mother made a 𝅘𝅥 to buy a bag of 🌸

A favorite with all ages, but particularly with youngsters who have difficulty with spelling, is creating a rebus story. Each student rewrites an episode in a story (or creates a new story), substituting pictures for some of the words. (Skills: comprehension, critical thinking)

A Roller Movie (I or G; art, speaking)

Each student or small group of students can use a roller movie to retell a story. First, they paint or draw scenes from the story on a long strip of butcher paper (the scenes should be original ones, not ones copied from the book). Each end of the paper is fastened to a piece of doweling or a broom handle so that the paper can unroll like a scroll. Then they make boxes for their movies. An opening a little smaller than the picture is cut out of the bottom of a cardboard box, which is turned on its side. The rollers go into holes at the top and bottom of the sides of the box. One student can narrate the story while another student turns the rollers. (Skills: comprehension, sequencing, critical thinking, visual imaging)

Scene Locations (I or G; art, writing)

Ask students to imagine that a movie is to be made of a book they have just read—and they have been asked to find locations for the filming. Identifying and describing or drawing the various locales in the book will require a thorough knowledge of the story. (Skills: comprehension, critical thinking, visual imaging)

88

89

90

Sequels (I; writing)

91 Each student writes a sequel to a book he or she has read. This requires a thorough familiarity with the motivations and backgrounds of the characters. Adding the sequel to the school library is an excellent motivation for this creative writing assignment. As the culmination to this activity, invite a real author to share the results.
(Skills: comprehension, vocabulary building, character analysis, creative writing)

Solution Letters (I; writing)

92 Each student writes a letter to a character in a book with advice about how he or she might have gotten out of a predicament or solved a problem. The proposed solution must be appropriate for the character to whom the letter is written.
(Skills: comprehension, character analysis)

A Story Frieze (G; art)

93 To illustrate a story, students create a frieze with crayon or tempera paint depicting scenes in sequence. These may be drawn on a long strip of butcher paper, or individual pictures can be mounted as a frieze. Pictures should be large enough to be seen easily when mounted high on the wall.
(Skills: sequencing, comprehension)

Story Illustrations (I; art, writing)

94 With crayons, paint, cut paper, or a combination of media, each student creates a picture of an event in a selected story and writes a brief description of the scene. Before beginning the picture, it will be helpful if the student thinks about the atmosphere of the scene and lists the words the author uses to describe the scene and to create its atmosphere.
(Skills: comprehension, visual imaging, critical thinking)

Story Mapping (CE; discussion)

95 After a story has been read aloud and discussed, ask questions about each of the main elements of the story: leading characters, setting, problem, steps to solve the problem, and the final solution. List these elements on the

chalkboard in a diagrammatic form that presents a clear picture of the plot. This activity will enable learners to recognize the internal structure of a story.
(Skills: comprehension, plot analysis)

Story Panels (I; art)

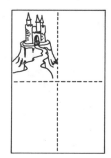

This activity gives nonverbal students the chance to express themselves in pictures. It is also an excellent activity for oral book reports. To begin their story panels, the students fold 12-by-18-inch pieces of drawing paper into four equal panels. Then they draw and color a scene in each panel. The panels should be sequential, and each panel should illustrate something that happened in the story rather than just depict an object. When they are done, students explain their drawings to their classmates.
(Skills: comprehension, visual imaging)

96

Story Update (I; writing)

97

Each student rewrites a story (or an episode) set in an earlier time as it might happen today.
(Skills: comprehension, creative writing)

A Student Book Jacket (I; art)

98

After a student has written an original story (or a follow-up chapter, an added incident, or a sequel to a book), he or she designs a book jacket for it.
(Skills: comprehension, visual imaging)

Taped Review (I; speaking)

99

Students tape-record book reviews instead of writing them. They should be careful to divulge enough about the book to arouse the interest of the listener but not so much that they spoil the story for a prospective reader.

Remind them that all reviews need not be favorable. But whether the review is favorable or unfavorable, the reasons why the reader liked or did not like the book must be explained.
(Skills: critical thinking, character analysis, plot analysis)

Telegram Reports (I; writing)

100 Each student pretends to be a reporter who sends a telegram to the newspaper describing an event in a selected story. This is a good exercise in summarizing the main idea, because a telegram must use as few words as possible.
(Skills: comprehension, critical thinking)

Then and Now/There and Here (I; art)

101 From a story set in a different time or country, draw a pair of pictures showing an event in the story and what the event would look like if it happened in this country today.
(Skills: comprehension, visual imaging)

This Is Your Life (G; speaking, reading)

102 Students plan a "This Is Your Life" program for a book character or an author. The program can be recorded on tape and played for critique and discussion or for a special program for parents or for another class.
(Skills: research, oral expression)

Three-dimensional Picture Map (I or G; art)

103 Using cut paper, paint, small objects, and other materials (such as bits of sponge for trees), each student or group of students creates a three-dimensional picture map of the locale of a book or story.
(Skills: comprehension, visual imaging)

The Three W's (I; writing; discussion)

104 After a book has been read aloud or a group of students have independently read the same book or story, each of them makes a chart with the headings Who, What, and Where. The characters in the book are listed under Who; the important objects are listed under What; and the locales are listed under Where. Under each of these subheadings, the student lists as many relevant descriptive words as possible. Lists should be shared and discussed. Here's an example:

WHO	WHAT	WHERE
Tommy	castle	on the hill
puzzled	old	high
kind	crumbly	barren

(Skills: vocabulary building, comprehension)

105

A Time Line (I or G; reading, art)
Books that extend over a period of time—such as historical stories, biographies, or novels that chronicle someone's life—lend themselves well to the construction of time lines on which each event or stage is recorded or pictured.
(Skills: sequencing, comprehension)

106

Twenty Questions (G; reading, discussion)
Several students leave the room while the remainder select a book title and author. The group returns and tries to identify the book by asking twenty questions.
(Skills: comprehension, critical thinking)

107

TV Anchor Report (I, G; writing, speaking)
Students pretend they are TV anchors. Each one selects an event from a book to be included in a newscast and writes a news script about it, using only the salient points and a few interesting details.

ACTION NEWS

This activity can be expanded into a full-fledged newscast during which the anchor calls on reporters reporting from various locations. One report might come from a science fiction enthusiast, another from a student who enjoys historical novels, and yet another from a "reporter" who likes to read about other countries. And think of the report that could be based on one of the events in *From the Mixed-up Files of Mrs. Basil E. Frankweiler.* Younger children can describe events in books such as *Charlotte's Web, The Wizard of Oz,* or *Charlie and the Chocolate Factory.*
(Skills: comprehension, creative writing, critical thinking)

Wide Reading (I; art)

Using a black felt pen, each student draws a continuous-line doodle on a large sheet of paper. Be sure the doodle has at least ten spaces. Each space is then labeled with a different category of reading material, such as adventure, mystery, biography, and historical novel. After the student reads a particular type of book, he or she colors in the appropriate space. The result of sampling each reading category will be a psychedelic design.
(Skills: knowledge of book categories)

108

Write It as a Poem (I; writing)

After some study of poetry, each student writes a poem about an event, a character, a place, or an object in a selected story. The poem might even be a critique of the story!

Students can prepare their poems for display by neatly printing each poem in the middle of an 11-by-18-inch sheet of drawing paper and surrounding it with appropriate sketches and designs. (For more ideas about teaching poetry, see activities 112–127.)
(Skill: creative writing)

109

"Why" Stories (I; writing)

After reading and discussing such folk stories as "Why the Oak Tree Never Loses Its Leaves" or "Why the Bear Is Stumpy-Tailed," each student composes an original "why" (or "pourquoi") story. (For more ideas about teaching folk stories, see activities 128–139.)
(Skill: creative writing)

110

You Are There (I; writing)

Each student assumes the role of a radio or TV reporter and describes an exciting event in a story in a "You Are There" format. The "reporter" should vividly describe the scene and should create interviews with participants in and witnesses to the event. Students may be interested to know that this classic TV format is being revived.
(Skills: comprehension, creative writing)

111

POETRY ACTIVITIES

Before beginning any poetry activity, students should have an opportunity to listen to many poems read by someone who does it well. One of the reasons we enjoy poetry is the beauty of the language; thus when we are introducing poetry to children, we need to pay special attention to how it sounds. Many fine cassettes of poetry readings are available, but poetry read aloud by the teacher or by a student who reads and interprets well is the most effective approach.

After the children have listened to, read, shared, and discussed a number of poems, expand their learning with any of the following activities.

112

Bulletin Board Display (CE)
Create a bulletin board display of favorite poems. Some may be illustrated.
(Skill: poetry appreciation)

113

Choral Reading (G; reading, speaking)
Divide the class into small groups, and divide a poem into different voices, with each group reading an assigned part. It is easiest to begin with alternate verses read by two groups. Later, you can assign children to groups according to the pitch of their voice (high, low), and you can divide poems according to meaning. Some books on teaching poetry contain poems that are divided for choral reading (see Bibliography, pages 94–95).
(Skills: fluency, comprehension; poetry appreciation)

114

Class Notebook of Favorite Poems (I, CE; art)
Each child submits a favorite poem, with an original illustration and his or her name, for a class notebook.
(Skill: poetry appreciation)

115

Class Poem (G; writing)
Compose a class poem about an event, a story the class has read, a favorite book or author, or any favorite subject.
(Skill: creative writing)

Color Poems (I, CE; art, writing)

116 Read Mary O'Neill's "Hailstones and Halibut Bones" and other poems about color. Have students illustrate them with fingerpaints or watercolors or look for pictures that illustrate the poems. Have them create original "color" poems.

Create a bulletin board display of color poems, pictures, and student illustrations.
(Skills: comprehension, creative writing)

Dramatize a Poem (G; dramatic expression)

117 Students dramatize a narrative poem in pantomime while a narrator reads the poem. Or they can dramatize the poem by creating dialogue in appropriate places.
(Skill: comprehension; poetry appreciation)

Favorite Poet (I; research)

118 Each student researches the life and work of a favorite poet and makes a scrapbook of pictures, poems, and the story of the poet's life. Have a poet's day to share the findings.
(Skill: critical thinking)

Glossary of Poetic Expressions (G; reading, discussion)

119 Develop an ongoing glossary of beautiful poetic expressions, particularly descriptive poetic phrases, on a large sheet of paper with a felt pen nearby. Children can add to the glossary as they read by themselves, or the glossary can be built by class discussion.
(Skills: comprehension, vocabulary building; poetry appreciation)

Illustrated Poems (I; art)

120 There are many ways for students to illustrate a poem that they have copied:
- with a picture done with crayons, watercolors, or fingerpaint,
- with a colored border around the poem centered on a 9-by-12-inch piece of paper, or

- with a beautiful or interesting object or picture they have found.

The found picture or object can also be used to inspire the writing of a poem. (Skills: comprehension, critical thinking, creative writing)

121

Limericks (I; writing)
Students enjoy writing humorous limericks following the rhyme scheme *a a b b a*. Here's an example:

> There was an old man with a beard,
> Who said, "It is just as I feared!
> Two owls and a hen,
> Four larks and a wren
> Have all built nests in my beard."

(Skill: creative writing)

122

Poems about Special Interests (I; research, art)
Each child finds poems about a subject of particular interest and illustrates some of the poems with pictures from magazines and original art. The student can also look for cassette recordings of any of the poems or about any of the poets. When all the material is gathered, students share their findings with the rest of the class. (Skills: comprehension, critical thinking; poetry appreciation)

123

Poems for Special Days (I; writing)

Commemorate a special day or event—such as Mother's Day, Father's Day, or Christmas—with a poem. (Skill: creative writing)

124

Poet of the Month (I, CE; reading, writing, art)
Select a poet of the month. Display some of his or her poems and pictures illustrating them and the poet's life. Play cassette recordings of the poems or about the life of the poet. Have the children read aloud and illustrate some of the poems. After discussion of the poet's style, have them try writing a poem in that style. Select a class favorite for special display. (Skills: comprehension, creative writing; poetry appreciation)

Poetry Festival (G; speaking)

125 Hold a poetry festival where everyone reads his or her favorite poem.
(Skills: fluency; poetry appreciation)

Prose and Poetry (I; writing)

126 To help students understand the difference between prose and poetry, let them rewrite a narrative poem as a prose story. Or they can rewrite events in a story (or the whole story) as a narrative poem. Or they can write a poem to describe a favorite character in a story.
(Skills: creative writing; poetry appreciation)

Real Versus Fanciful Language (CE; reading)

127 Keep an ongoing chart of real and fanciful language. Use pictures to add interest and clarify the differences. Your chart might begin like this:

Real	Fanciful
boy	elf
horse	unicorn
girl	fairy

(Skills: comprehension, vocabulary building)

Recommended Poetry Books

Adams, Adrienne. *Poetry of Earth and Sky*. New York: Scribner, 1972.

Adoff, Arnold. *All the Colors of the Race*. New York: Lothrop, 1982.

Aldis, Dorothy. *All Together*. New York: Putnam, 1952.

Bierhorst, John, ed. *In the Trail of the Wind: American Indian Poems and Ritual Orations*. New York: Farrar, Straus and Giroux, 1971.

———, ed. *The Ring in the Prairie*. New York: Dial, 1976.

Blishen, Edward, ed. *Oxford Book of Poetry for Children*. Salem: Merrimack, 1984.

Brewton, Sara, and John Brewton, eds. *America Forever New: A Book of Poems*. New York: Crowell, 1968.

Ciardi, John. *You Read to Me, I'll Read to You*. Philadelphia: Lippincott, 1961.

Cole, William, ed. *Poem Stew*. New York: Harper & Row, 1983.

Daniel, Mark. *A Child's Treasury of Poems*. New York: Dial, 1986.

de Gerez, Toni. *My Song Is a Piece of Jade: Poems of Ancient Mexico in English and Spanish*. Boston: Little Brown, 1984.

Fisher, Aileen. *Out in the Dark and Daylight*. New York: Harper & Row, 1980.

Hopkins, Lee B., ed. *Don't You Turn Back*. New York: Knopf, 1969.

Larrick, Nancy, ed. *Crazy to Be Alive in Such a Strange World*. New York: M. Evans, 1977.

———, ed. *Piping Down the Valleys Wild*. New York: Dell, 1982.

———. *When the Dark Comes Dancing*. New York: Philomel, 1983.

Lear, Edward. *How Pleasant to Know Mr. Lear!* New York: Holiday, 1982.

Martin, Bill, Jr., John Archambault, and Peggy Brogan. *Bill Martin Jr.'s Treasure Chest of Poetry*. New York: DLM Teaching Resources, 1986.

Merriam, Eve. *There Is No Rhyme for Silver*. New York: Atheneum, 1962.

O'Neill, Mary. *Hailstones and Halibut Bones*. New York: Doubleday, 1961.

THE THEMATIC APPROACH

The thematic approach to teaching literature is one of the most effective techniques for involving everyone in the class, regardless of reading level, in the same language arts program. It simply means selecting a theme around which language arts activities can be developed. Once a theme has been selected, everyone can read books and stories on his or her reading level and all can participate in the discussions, sharing periods, and creative activities. Whether the theme is folk tales, sports, science fiction, or fantasy, you should be able to find worthwhile books for all levels. Within the scope of the thematic approach there is opportunity to develop reading, writing, speaking, and listening skills within a functional setting. Such mechanics are important to you, the teacher, but more important is that in following a theme your students will enjoy reading many books, learning research methods, and expanding their language arts skills.

To summarize, the thematic approach can

1. teach language arts skills in a meaningful setting,
2. cut across groups and allow for equal contribution by all students,
3. provide functional use of language arts skills,
4. provide activities to meet the needs of all students,
5. help to promote individual responsibility by providing alternatives and options in materials to be read, forms of presentation for sharing, and creative projects to be developed,
6. offer unlimited opportunities for students to read for enjoyment as well as with a purpose in mind, and
7. widen a student's horizons by introducing a broad spectrum of literature.

"It sounds great," you say, "but how do we go about it?" Let us take it step by step.

Step 1: Select a Theme
This is the most vital step of the procedure. The theme should be based on student interest. It may develop from a story that has been read, a TV program, a study trip, a picture, an object of particular interest, an event, or a special person. An alert teacher can usually wait and watch for an appropriate subject. Sometimes in the interest of broadening horizons, however, the teacher must motivate interest in a particular theme. No matter how the selection is made, the theme should be a subject that arouses the

interest of the students and has the potential for interesting research and activities.

Before you plunge in, there's one more thing to do. Be sure that adequate material related to the theme is available. It can be devastating to suddenly discover after exciting the students that the library has only three books on the subject!

Step 2: Prepare Your Resources
Finding books on the selected theme isn't difficult if you seek out sources. First, of course, is the school librarian. Enlist her help in setting up a special display of books related to your theme. Then visit the book room in your school. Book rooms are always great sources of books on all reading levels. No matter how old they are, basal readers, supplementary readers, and literature books contain many fine selections from the best of children's literature. Select a wide variety of books at different reading levels that have stories related to your theme. Pick up several copies of the same book so that children can read together and discuss the stories. These books can form the nucleus of your room library.

Ask the students to contribute any books they may have on the theme. Another good source is Friends of the Library book sales. Flea markets, too, often have interesting books to offer. This is a good way to spend that PTA money.

Ask your school librarian to give a book talk or story hour related to your theme as an opening salvo. If your school does not have a librarian, contact the local children's librarian. They welcome these kinds of requests. And if all else fails, do the book talk or story hour yourself!

Step 3: Have the Students Read Widely
Once you have introduced the theme, encourage the students to select books on the subject at their own reading level. This does not have to be put into so many words. A suggestion to read, in the interest of research, any interesting book that is at all related to the subject usually makes everyone comfortable choosing books at his or her own level.

Schedule ample reading times during this period so that you will be available to consult or advise.

Step 4: Encourage Students to Share Stories
This is an enjoyable time. Encourage students to share their reading in a variety of ways, such as reading a part of a story aloud, retelling a story with flannelboard figures, or dramatizing a scene. Such sharing may result in a panel of students who have

read the same book discussing likenesses and differences in characters, or it may stimulate further research on the topic.

From their reading and research, help the students to formulate generalizations and to recognize special characteristics of various types of literature, such as folk tales, science fiction, fantasy, biography, or mystery. Teachers' manuals that accompany literature readers and children's literature anthologies are excellent sources of this type of information.

Step 5: Offer Enjoyable Activities

Students can participate in a variety of creative activities as they present their interpretations of stories they have read. These activities may include dramatizations, displays, dioramas, picto-maps, murals, panel discussions, and interviews. It is usually advisable to set a deadline for the completion of activities to maintain the interest level.

Each of the following theme sections contains activities specifically appropriate to the theme. These may be augumented, however, by any of the general activities (1–112).

Step 6: Pull It All Together

Plan an activity that provides students with a vehicle for displaying what they have learned and for culminating the study. This final step may be a presentation to parents and friends or to another class, or it may be an exhibition for the school or local library.

THEMATIC ACTIVITIES

FOLK STORIES

Having long been a favorite with children of all ages, folk stories are an excellent subject for theme development. As children read a variety of folk tales, they will notice that the same story appears in slightly different versions in many countries. These similarities may be due to folk stories having been passed on orally by many generations of storytellers, or they may be due to the common subject of folk stories, namely, human foibles. The children will also notice that certain motifs recur in many folk tales, such as the magic number three, trickery, wishes, magic objects, and animals that talk. Some authorities have divided folk stories into three major categories: animals that talk, tales about everyday people, and fairy tales. The literature reader Wider Than the Sky *(Margaret Early, ed.) lists the characteristics of folk tales:*

1. rapidly moving action,
2. vague setting (in a faraway country),
3. simple characterization,
4. repetition of basic ideas,
5. contrasted values (strong versus weak, wise versus foolish)
6. standardized techniques of fantasy (magic, giants, etc.),
7. language with distinctive qualities.

Before embarking on any of the suggested activities, the students should read and discuss a wide variety of folk stories. These activities can, of course, be supplemented with any of the general activities (1–112).

47

128 Arrange an **exhibit of folk story anthologies.**

129 Collect **different versions of the same story.** Have your students compare and discuss possible reasons for likenesses and differences.

130 With your students' help, gather and display **samples of folklore figures** such as dwarfs, trolls, dragons, elves, and animals.
   The children can write an original folk story about any three figures in the collection.

131 Have the students **dramatize folk tales** using paper-bag masks they have constructed. They can perform the folk tales for another grade, and let that class guess the titles.

132 Have your students each draw and color a **sequential series of pictures** illustrating a folk tale.

133 Arrange for your class to **tell a folk story to a lower grade.** Practice it thoroughly beforehand.

134 Organize a **folk-storytelling festival.** Encourage the students to use flannelboard figures, puppets, roller movies, and other media.
   Seek out local storytellers and invite them to participate in your festival, or just to present a story hour.

135 Create a **frieze around the room** depicting scenes from folk tales.

136 Make a **poster** showing the characteristics of folk tales.

137 Your students **create their own "tall tales."** On four separate slips of paper, write down who did what, where, and why in familiar folk stories. Label four boxes Who, What, Where, and Why. Put the slips of paper in the appropriate boxes. To make a story each child selects one slip of paper from each box and places them in the correct order. Each child then reads his or her story aloud. Small children especially like this activity because the stories are usually quite silly. For example,

"The bumblebee baked a cake in a cave to kill the dragon" or "The red fox flew away at the North Pole to play baseball."

138 Help students to conduct **research on beliefs we have today** that stem from folklore. This research correlates well with studies of American Indians, Eskimos, Aztecs, Incas, and people in various regions of the United States.

139 After reading a story that contains fantasy, students fill in a sheet with **two columns: one labeled "Could Happen" and the other labeled "Make-Believe."** The teacher may wish to demonstrate first on the chalkboard with a story familiar to everyone. This is an especially effective activity for young children, who may sometimes have difficulty differentiating between real and make-believe.

Recommended Folk Story Books

Ahlberg, Janet, and Allen Ahlberg. *The Jolly Postman, or Other People's Letters.* Boston: Little Brown, 1986.

Baskin, Leonard. *Imps, Demons, Hobgoblins, Witches, Fairies and Elves.* New York: Pantheon, 1984.

Brown, Marcia. *Stone Soup.* New York: Scribner, 1947.

Carpenter, Frances. *African Wonder Tales.* New York: Doubleday, 1963.

Chase, Richard. *The Complete Tales of Uncle Remus.* Boston: Houghton Mifflin, 1955.

D'Aulaire, Ingri, and Edgar D'Aulaire. *D'Aulaire's Trolls.* New York: Doubleday, 1972.

Dayrell, Elphinstone. *Why the Sun and the Moon Live in the Sky.* Boston: Houghton Mifflin, 1977.

de la Mare, Walter. *Tales Told Again.* New York: Knopf, 1961.

Downing, Charles. *Tales of the Hodja.* Portland: Walck, 1965.

Griego, Margot C., et al. *Tortillitas para Mamá: And Other Spanish Nursery Rhymes.* New York: Holt, Rinehart and Winston, 1981.

Grimm, Jakob, and Wilhelm Grimm. *The Bremen Town Musicians.* Morristown: Silver, 1985.

Hamilton, Virginia. *The People Could Fly: American Black Folktales.* New York: Knopf, 1985.

Hautien, Cheng. *Six Chinese Brothers: An Ancient Tale.* New York: Holt, 1979.

Hume, Lotta. *Favorite Children's Stories from Tibet and China.* Tokyo: Tuttle, 1962.

Keats, Ezra J. *John Henry: An American Legend.* New York: Pantheon, 1965.

McDermott, Gerald. *Anansi the Spider: A Tale from the Ashanti.* New York: Holt, Rinehart and Winston, 1972.

———. *Arrow to the Sun: A Pueblo Indian Tale.* New York: Viking, 1974.

Rice, Eve. *Once in a Wood: Ten Tales from Aesop.* New York: Greenwillow, 1979.

Uchida, Yoshiko. *Magic Listening Cap: More Folk Tales from Japan.* New York: Harcourt Brace Jovanovich: 1965.

Van Duong, Quyen, and Jewell R. Coburn. *Beyond the East Wind: Legends and Folktales of Vietnam.* Thousand Oaks: Burn, Hart, 1976.

MODERN FANTASY

After introducing the theme, encourage wide reading in books of modern (in comparison to traditional folk and fairy tales) fantasy. Discuss the various types of fantasy. Charlotte Huck classifies modern fantasy in the following categories:

1. strange and curious worlds *(The Phantom Tollbooth),*
2. imaginary kingdoms *(The Lion, the Witch and the Wardrobe),*
3. animal fantasy *(Stuart Little),*
4. the world of toys and dolls *(The Adventures of Pinocchio),*
5. Lilliputian worlds *(The Borrowers),*
6. fabulous flights *(James and the Giant Peach),*
7. magical powers *(Half Magic),*

8. overcoming evil *(An Enemy at Green Knowe),*
9. science fiction *(A Wrinkle in Time)*

Students may wish to create new categories as their discussions progress and they assign the books they have read to the various classifications. Wide reading is important before embarking on the suggested activities, although some of them will also require further reading and rereading.

140 Create a **bulletin board display** of examples of fantasy—pictures, drawings, and stories.

141 Have your students **write an original story** creating a new world with fantastic happenings and imaginary people and creatures. Detailed descriptions, distinctive characteristics, and appropriate names are especially important. Or they might write a story using the type of fantasy found in a favorite story. This story may be a group or a partner project, if desired. Some students may like to tell their story to a lower grade using flannelboard characters.
  They can also **create creatures and people** from the "new world" out of clay, papier-mâché, or paper sculpture, or simply draw and color them. Each creature should be labeled with a name and description.

142 Plan and develop a **mural** (preferably 3-D) depicting a fantasy world. Include plants, animals, people, houses, and modes of transportation. Tempera paint alone or combined with cut paper is an effective medium.

143 Students **dramatize several scenes** from fantasy stories. The scenes selected should be complete in themselves so that they will be understandable to the audience.

144 Help your students **research the life of an author** of fantasy, such as Lloyd Alexander, J. R. R. Tolkien, or Roald Dahl.

145 Class members make **mobiles** of objects from a story they have read or from the "new world" created in No. 141. Mobiles are easily constructed from wire coat hangers and thin wire, yarn, string or thread of various lengths.

146 **Invite an author** of fantasy to speak to the class about writing a fantasy story. Students might like to share their own stories with a real author.

147 **Collect stories** that are examples of the different types of fantasy.

Recommended Modern Fantasy Books

Alexander, Lloyd. *The Illyrian Adventure*. New York: Dutton, 1986.

———. *Taran Wanderer*. New York: Holt, Rinehart and Winston, 1967.

Berenstain, Michael. *The Dwarks at the Mall*. New York: Bantam/Skylark, 1985.

Bishop, Claire. *The Five Chinese Brothers*. New York: Coward, 1938.

Boston, L. M. *The Children of Green Knowe*. New York: Harcourt Brace Jovanovich, 1955.

Dahl, Roald. *James and the Giant Peach*. New York: Knopf: 1961.

Eager, Edgar. *Half Magic*. New York: Harcourt Brace Jovanovich, 1985.

Grahame, Kenneth. *The Wind in the Willows*. New York: Scribner, 1933.

Hunter, Mollie. *The Three Day Enchantment*. New York: Harper & Row, 1985.

Juster, Norton. *The Phantom Tollbooth*. New York: Random, 1961.

Kahl, Virginia. *The Duchess Bakes a Cake*. New York: Scribner, 1955.

Lawson, Robert. *Rabbit Hill*. New York: Viking, 1944.

L'Engle, Madeline. *A Wrinkle in Time*. New York: Farrar, Straus and Giroux, 1962.

Lewis, C. S. *The Lion, the Witch and the Wardrobe*. New York: Macmillan, 1950.

Lindbergh, Anne. *Bailey's Window*. New York: Harcourt Brace Jovanovich, 1984.

Norton, Mary. *The Borrowers*. New York: Harcourt Brace Jovanovich, 1953.

O'Brien, Robert. *Mrs. Frisby and the Rats of NIMH*. New York: Atheneum, 1971.

Seldon, George. *The Cricket in Times Square*. Farrar, Straus and Giroux, 1960.

Seuss, Dr. *And to Think I Saw It on Mulberry Street*. New York: Vanguard, 1937.

Tolkien, J. R. R. *The Hobbit*. Boston: Houghton Mifflin, 1982.

White, E. B. *Charlotte's Web*. New York: Harper & Row, 1952.
——. *Stuart Little*. New York: Harper & Row, 1945.

ANIMALS THAT TALK

Stories about animals that talk are a perennial favorite with all ages. To the joy of younger children, storybooks abound with them, and older students find pleasure in the antics of Toad and the adventures of Mrs. Frisby. Readers are fascinated with animals that talk because they often can recognize themselves and people they know in these characters. Another delight of reading this kind of story is that it often mirrors our society, and students smile as they recognize a familiar conversation or situation. Stories about talking animals usually combine the elements of humor, fantasy, and action, and they offer many possibilities for interesting activities.

148 Arrange a **display of storybooks** about animals that talk. These may be as simple as *The Three Bears,* or as complex as *The Wind in the Willows*. Discuss these stories and why they were written.
   Then have the children put together an **exhibit of stuffed and toy animals** and puppets. They can select two or three to use as characters in a story, or one favorite about which to write a "biography."

149 Develop a subunit on the **life and stories of Beatrix Potter.**

150 Draw and color **flannelboard characters** for retelling a story. You might paint three different backdrops—

city, farm, and country—on flannel cloth to throw over the flannelboard. Have the children select the appropriate scene for the background of their stories.

151 Play **cassettes** by noted storytellers, and show **filmstrips and videotapes** of animal stories.

152 Students **illustrate stories** with crayons, fingerpaints, tempera, or watercolors. Be sure they label their pictures.

153 Develop a **frieze** around the room showing scenes from animal stories.

154 Each student writes an original **"pourquoi" (why) story,** such as "Why the Bluejay Screeches" or "Why the Fox Has a Bushy Tail."

155 Have students **dramatize stories in pantomime** while a narrator reads.

156 Students make **mobiles** with objects from a favorite story.

157 Let students **create "new animals."** First they draw or color figures of animals on colored paper. Then they cut each animal in half between the head and the hind part. Next they each choose one front half and one back half and mount them on construction paper to create an original creature. More elaborate new animals may be constructed from papier-mâché or clay and painted interesting colors. Whether your class's animals are plain or fancy, part of the fun is thinking up an original name for each new creature.

Recommended Books about Animals That Talk

Bond, Michael. *A Bear Called Paddington*. Boston: Houghton Mifflin, 1958.
Brooks, Walter R. *Freddy the Detective*. New York: Knopf, 1987.
Eastman, P. D. *Are You My Mother?* New York: Random, 1960.
Fatio, Louise. *The Happy Lion*. New York: McGraw-Hill, 1964.
Galdone, Paul. *The Little Red Hen*. Boston: Houghton Mifflin, 1985.

──────. *The Three Billy Goats Gruff*. Boston: Houghton Mifflin, 1981.

Grahame, Kenneth. *The Wind in the Willows*. New York: Scribner, 1933.

Green, Carol. *The Insignificant Elephant*. New York: Harcourt Brace Jovanovich, 1985.

Lionni, Leo. *Frederick*. New York: Pantheon, 1967.

McCloskey, Robert. *Make Way for Ducklings*. New York: Viking, 1941.

Milne, A. A. *Winnie the Pooh*. New York: Dutton, 1954.

Minarik, Else H. *Father Bear Comes Home*. New York: Harper & Row, 1959.

──────. *Little Bear*. New York: Harper & Row, 1957.

──────. *Little Bear's Friend*. New York: Harper & Row, 1960.

──────. *Little Bear's Visit*. New York: Harper & Row, 1961.

O'Brien, Robert. *Mrs. Frisby and the Rats of NIMH*. New York: Atheneum, 1971.

Potter, Beatrix. *The Tale of Peter Rabbit*. New York: Warne, 1981.

Rey, H. A. *Curious George*. Boston: Houghton Mifflin, 1941.

Seldon, George. *The Cricket in Times Square*. Farrar, Straus and Giroux, 1960.

Titus, Eve. *Anatole*. New York: McGraw Hill, 1956.

White, E. B. *Charlotte's Web*. New York: Harper & Row, 1952.

──────. *Stuart Little*. New York: Harper & Row, 1945.

FAMOUS PEOPLE (BIOGRAPHIES)

Students are usually interested in the lives of famous people. Have available a collection of biographies and autobiographies that represent a broad spectrum of fields of endeavor: statesmen, sports figures, entertainers, inventors, explorers, and so on. Discuss the

difference between biographies and autobiographies and the merits of each. These types of books are important because they help students to understand and appreciate their heritage. They also help the students to see that sometimes a goal is attained only through hardships and determination. Biographies are an effective means of presenting a true picture of history in a readable format. Begin the activities after laying a foundation of wide reading and discussion.

158 The class **discusses what makes a person famous.** Is *famous* the same as *great*?

159 Students each make a **picto-map** showing a selected person's life and accomplishments.

160 Hold a **"press conference"** or a series of interviews in which each student assumes the role of the person about whom they have read.

161 Students paint pictures for a **frieze** around the room depicting scenes from the lives of the people they have selected. These should be original pictures, not copies of other art.

162 Hold **roundtable discussions** among several "famous people" (played by the students). Each one can express his or her view on the subject under discussion or simply ask one another questions about his or her participation in particular events or endeavors. Students should prepare questions beforehand to make this activity effective.

163 Hold a **debate** between two "famous people" with opposing viewpoints.

164 Class members **dramatize scenes** from the lives of famous people. Or they can **present tableaus** of scenes, accompanied by a prepared narration.

165 Create a **bulletin board display** of pictures and articles about famous people and their accomplishments.

166 Students write the **biography of a classmate,** friend, relative, or local personality.

167

Writing alone or discussing in a group, students **compare the approaches and styles of authors** of biographies.

Recommended Biographies

Blythe, Randolph. *Amelia Earhart*. New York: Franklin Watts, 1987.

D'Aulaire, Ingri, and Edgar Parin D'Aulaire. *Columbus*. New York: Doubleday, 1987.

Evans, Mark. *Scott Joplin and the Ragtime Years*. New York: Dodd, Mead, 1976.

Faber, Doris. *Eleanor Roosevelt: First Lady of the World*. New York: Viking, 1985.

Franchere, Ruth. *Cesar Chavez*. New York: Harper & Row, 1973.

Freedman, Russell D. *Lincoln: A Photographic Biography*. Boston: Clarion, 1987.

Fritz, Jean. *And Then What Happened, Paul Revere?* New York: Putnam, 1973.

―――. *Where Was Patrick Henry on the 29th of May?* New York: Putnam: 1975.

Greenfeld, Howard. *Marc Chagall: An Introduction*. London: Ernest Benn, 1980.

Hale, Janet C. *The Owl's Song*. New York: Avon, 1976.

Hautzig, Esther. *Endless Steppe: A Girl in Exile*. New York: Harper & Row, 1987.

Hunter, Edith F. *Child of the Silent Night: The Story of Laura Bridgman*. Boston: Houghton Mifflin, 1983.

Huynh, Quang Nhuong. *Land I Lost: Adventures of a Boy in Vietnam*. New York: Harper & Row, 1982.

Jackson, Jesse. *Make a Joyful Noise unto the Lord: The Life of Mahalia Jackson, Queen of the Gospel Singers*. New York: Harper & Row, 1974.

Keller, Mollie. *Golda Meier*. New York: Franklin Watts, 1983.

Kroeber, Theodora. *Ishi, Last of His Tribe*. Boston: Houghton Mifflin, 1964.

Metzger, Larry. *Abraham Lincoln, A First Book*. New York: Franklin Watts, 1987.

Morrison, Dorothy N. *Under a Strong Wind: The Adventures of Jessie Benton Fremont*. New York: Macmillan, 1983.

O'Connor, Karen. *Sally Ride and the New Astronauts*. New York: Franklin Watts, 1983.

Quackenbush, Robert. *Mark Twain? What Kind of Name Is That? A Story of Samuel Langhorne Clemens*. Englewood Cliffs: Prentice-Hall, 1984.

Sandburg, Carl. *Abe Lincoln Grows Up*. New York: Harcourt Brace Jovanovich, 1926.

Taylor, Judy. *Beatrix Potter: Artist, Storyteller and Country Woman*. New York: Warne, 1986.

SURVIVAL

Students enjoy reading about characters who struggle against great odds to survive and in doing so portray unusual courage and fortitude or find an inner strength when the will to live conquers fear. Survival takes different forms; the goal may be to stay alive, to improve one's lot in life, to prove something, or to reach a particular place. Through reading survival stories, students may recognize that the characters first learn to accept reality and then embark on a strategy for survival. They may also recognize that many people find courage and the strength to survive in their belief in such basic values as honor, truth, and personal commitment. Books about survival are popular because they are almost always filled with suspense, action, and conflict. Books about many different kinds of survival should be available for reading and discussion before any activities are introduced.

168 Students collect and display newspaper and magazine **articles and pictures about contemporary examples of survival.**

169 Divide the class into two or more groups to prepare **dramatizations of a reporter or reporters interviewing characters** from the selected books after they survived their trials—for example, when Karana in *Island of the Blue Dolphins* arrives in Santa Barbara, or when Mafatu in *Call It Courage* returns home to his island. Reporters will need to review the book to plan the questions they will ask.

170 Each student writes **diary or log entries** for several days in the life of a character who survived an ordeal. Descriptive details are important.

171 Invite a **local resident who has survived a traumatic situation** to talk to the class. Students can take notes of the talk and write them up as a newspaper or magazine article. Then have them read their articles aloud to compare what each student heard and thought was important.

172 Show the **movie** of *Island of the Blue Dolphins* or of any other book that has been read and discussed. Compare the movie version with the book and discuss possible reasons for any changes. This activity can underscore the importance of reading the book to understand the author's story before seeing the movie version of it.

173 Stage an informal **meeting where several characters** from different survival books **share feelings and reactions.** Encourage students who assume the roles of characters to "be" that person. To do so, they need to thoroughly understand the character and the story.

174 Students write an **imaginary newspaper headline** announcing the survival of each of the characters about whom they have read.

175 Each student designs a large **poster** advertising a favorite survival story.

176 Students working alone or with a co-author **write an original survival story,** with illustrations.

177 Invite the **school psychologist** to discuss how people react to traumatic experiences and survive. Have the students prepare questions they would like to have answered, especially ones related to the stories they have read.

Recommended Books about Survival

Burnford, Sheila. *The Incredible Journey*. Boston: Little, Brown, 1961.

Byars, Betsy. *The Midnight Fox*. New York: Viking, 1968.

Clifford, Eth. *The Curse of the Moonraker*. Boston: Houghton Mifflin, 1977.

Day, Veronique. *Landslide*. New York: Dell, 1966.

Ellis, Ella T. *Roam the Wild Country*. New York: Atheneum, 1972.

Ellis, Mel. *The Wild Horse Killers*. New York: Holt, Rinehart & Winston, 1976.

George, Jean C. *Julie of the Wolves*. New York: Harper & Row, 1972.

———. *My Side of the Mountain*. New York: Dutton, 1959.

Holm, Anne. *North to Freedom*. New York: Harcourt Brace Jovanovich, 1974.

Holman, Felice. *Slake's Limbo*. New York: Scribner, 1974.

Houston, James. *Tikta Liktak*. New York: Harcourt Brace Jovanovich, 1965.

Hunt, Irene. *No Promises in the Wind*. New York: Ace, 1981.

Mazer, Harry. *Snow Bound*. New York: Dell, 1975.

O'Dell, Scott. *Island of the Blue Dolphins*. Boston: Houghton Mifflin, 1960.

Phleger, Marjorie. *Pilot Down, Presumed Dead*. New York: Harper & Row, 1975.

Roth, Arthur. *The Iceberg Hermit*. New York: Scholastic, 1976.

Sachs, Muriel. *Underdog*. New York: Doubleday, 1985.

Speare, Elizabeth George. *The Sign of the Beaver*. Boston: Houghton Mifflin, 1983.

Sperry, Armstrong. *Call It Courage*. New York: Macmillan, 1968.

Taylor, Theodore. *The Cay*. New York: Avon, 1977.

Trull, Patti. *On with My Life*. New York: Putnam, 1983.

CHILDREN OF OTHER CULTURES AND COUNTRIES

Today's multiethnic student population presents us with built-in motivation for developing this theme. Gather a collection of books that present many different cultures and countries, including those represented in the class if possible. Encourage the students to read stories of several countries or cultures. In discussions stress the similarities of people rather than the differences, although the differences cannot be ignored since they usually have a basis in the physical, political, or social life of the country or culture. Students who are from other lands or cultures or who have traveled may become valuable resources. The activities will be more meaningful if they are based on wide reading and insightful discussion.

178 Display a large **map of the world** so that your students can pin a flag (with book title) on the locale of each book they have read.

179 Create a **progressive bulletin board** to display drawings of the leading characters of each book read. The drawings should be labeled with the character's name and the book in which he or she appears.

180 Hold a **meeting of characters** from several books. Have the "actors" plan the questions and topics they will discuss. Emphasize the importance of familiarity with the characters and with the events and descriptions in the books.

181 Create a **mural** of scenes from stories of other cultures or countries, showing contrasts of dress and home life. A mural divided into interesting shapes is effective for this project.

182 Organize a series of **interviews with characters** from selected books. The "interviewer" will prepare questions and topics to be discussed. Both the interviewer and the character need to be thoroughly familiar with the book.
  The interview can also be with the authors of selected books. Advise students to consult a librarian for author information.

183 Invite someone from another culture or country—a parent, a local resident, or a student who has recently come to this country—to share his or her experience. Try to find people who come from countries about which the students have been reading so that they can compare what they have read with what they hear.

184 Students **write a letter** to one of their favorite characters. Then they exchange letters with someone who has read the same book and answer the letter by assuming the role of the character.

185 Groups who have read the same book **dramatize a scene** or scenes from it. Emphasize the importance of interpreting the roles as described by the author. This activity can serve as the springboard for a discussion of the characters and their motivations.
   A variation is to have the group expand the dramatization to a then-what-might-have-happened scene, or one scene beyond the end of the story. This activity requires close attention to how the characters would act.

186 To culminate this theme of other cultures and countries, hold **a party** in which students attend in the role of their favorite book characters. Several students could serve as hosts acting as themselves. Encourage students to become, and not just pretend to be, the characters they have selected. They can assume the role in dress and in personality as expressed through conversation, actions, and reactions. In portraying people from other cultures, your students will gain a better understanding of them and of ideas that may be different from ours.

Recommended Books about Other Cultures and Countries

Buck, Pearl. *The Big Wave.* New York: Day, 1948.
Chauncy, Nan. *Devil's Hill.* New York: Franklin Watts, 1960.
Clark, Ann Nolan. *Secret of the Andes.* New York: Viking, 1952.
DeJong, Meindert. *The Wheel on the School.* New York: Harper & Row, 1954.
Gates, Doris. *Blue Willow.* New York: Viking, 1940.
Griffiths, Helen. *The Greyhound.* New York: Harcourt, 1973.
Hamilton, Virginia. *Zeely.* New York: Macmillan, 1967.
Handforth, Thomas. *Mei Li.* New York: Doubleday, 1938.
Hillerman, Tony. *Dance Hall of the Dead.* New York: Avon, 1975.

Krumgold, Joseph. ...*And Now Miguel*. New York: Crowell, 1953.

Lewis, Elizabeth Foreman. *Young Fu of the Upper Yangtze*. New York: Holt, Rinehart and Winston, 1960.

Lindgren, Astrid. *Pippi Longstocking*. New York: Viking, 1950.

McSwigan, Marie. *Snow Treasure*. New York: Dutton, 1964.

O'Dell, Scott. *The Black Pearl*. Boston: Houghton Mifflin, 1967.

————. *Child of Fire*. Boston: Houghton Mifflin, 1974.

Politi, Leo. *Three Stalks of Corn*. New York: Scribner, 1976.

Seredy, Kate. *The Good Master*. New York: Viking, 1935.

Shotwell, Louisa R. *Roosevelt Grady*. New York: Philomel, 1963.

Sommerfelt, Aimee. *Road to Agra*. New York: Criterion, 1964.

————. *The White Bungalow*. New York: Criterion, 1964.

Spyri, Johanna. *Heidi*. New York: Knopf, 1984.

Vander Els, Betty. *The Bomber's Moon*. New York: Farrar, Straus and Giroux, 1986.

MONSTERS, DRAGONS, AND SUCH

This is a favorite theme with all ages. Prepare a display of books about various kinds of monsters, dragons, and other mythical creatures. Encourage the students to read a number of books about different kinds of creatures so that they will have a basis for comparisons. Discuss the significance of monsters and dragons in folk stories and fantasy: how they are introduced to represent evil, or a harsh overlord, or perhaps a hard problem to overcome. Talk about the good monsters and dragons and how they might represent the lonely one, the ugly one, or the unwanted one. Help students to be aware that monsters and dragons in literature usually are endowed with human characteristics and often allegorically solve human problems. The activities should not be attempted until wide reading and discussion has taken place.

187 Have the class construct a **chart of the characteristics** of some of the most common supernatural creatures found in literature.

188 Collect and display **pictures and examples** of monsters, dragons, and such.

189 Students **create original monsters** with clay or papier-mâché, or draw them on large paper with crayon, paint, colored chalk, or fingerpaint. Each monster should have a distinctive name and be accompanied by a detailed description of the monster's unique characteristics. The elaborateness of these monsters will depend on the grade level of your students.

Have each child **write a story** about one of these original creations (they will probably want to write about their own).

190 In groups or individually, students construct **dioramas** of scenes in stories about monsters or dragons. They should accompany each diorama with a written description of the scene and the name of the story from which it comes.

191 Have a **"monster" parade,** where the children wear masks made of papier-mâché, paper bags, or other material. After the parade, each "monster" can tell its name and give a short oral description or autobiography.

192 Each child **writes a story about a meeting of two creatures** from different books. They will need to be very familiar with the two books to do this activity.

193 The class or groups of students **dramatize several monster stories** and use the masks they created for their parade. Select stories of both good and bad monsters.

194 Students create an attractive **scrapbook** of "My Favorite Monsters and Dragons." Each picture would have a name and description and the reason for being selected as a favorite.

195 Students **draw and color scenes from stories** about different mythical beasts. The pictures can be fastened together as a book or as a frieze-type wall decoration. Interesting pictures usually show some kind of action. A label identifying each creature and the story from which the scene was taken is helpful to the viewer.

Recommended Books about Monsters, Dragons, and Such

Bulla, Clyde. *My Friend the Monster*. New York: Crowell, 1980.

Child Study Association of America. *Castles and Dragons*. New York: Crowell-Collier, 1958.

Coville, Bruce. *The Monster's Ring*. New York: Pantheon, 1982.

Crowe, Robert L. *Clyde Monster*. New York: Dutton, 1976.

Galdone, Paul. *Monster and the Tailor*. Boston: Houghton Mifflin, 1982.

Lang, Andrew. *The Blue Fairy Book*. New York: Viking, 1978.

LeGuin, Ursula. *A Wizard of Earthsea*. New York: Houghton Mifflin, 1968.

McCaffrey, Anne. *Dragondrums*. New York: Atheneum, 1979.

———. *Dragonsinger*. New York: Atheneum, 1977.

———. *Dragonsong*. New York: Atheneum, 1976.

Mayer, Mercer. *The Lovesick Dragon*. New York: Macmillan, 1986.

Meddaugh, Susan. *Too Many Monsters*. Boston: Houghton Mifflin, 1982.

Nesbit, Edith. *The Complete Book of Dragons*. New York: Macmillan, 1973.

Palmer, Robin. *Dragons, Unicorns and Other Magical Beasts*. New York: Walck, 1966.

Schultz, Sam. *101 Monster Jokes*. New York: Lerner, 1982.

Sendak, Maurice. *Where the Wild Things Are*. New York: Harper & Row, 1963.

Smith, Janice L. *Monster in the Third Dresser Drawer and Other Stories about Adam Joshua*. New York: Harper & Row, 1981.

Spicer, Dorothy Gladys. *13 Monsters*. New York: Coward McCann, 1964.

Tolkien, J. R. R. *The Hobbit*. Boston: Houghton Mifflin, 1984.

Yolen, Jane. *Dragon's Blood*. New York: Delacorte, 1982.

———. *Dragons and Dreams*. New York: Harper & Row, 1986.

Zaring, Jane. *The Return of the Dragon*. Boston: Houghton Mifflin, 1981.

PEOPLE WHO WRITE BOOKS

The lives of authors often tell us much about the kinds of books they write. As students become familiar with authors, their insight into and understanding of the authors' works increase—and this, in turn, contributes to their enjoyment. For example, anyone knowing Beatrix Potter's background can truly appreciate her stories. Students need to become acquainted with authors of worthwhile literature at a time when their tastes and values are in the formative stage. Thus it is our task to expose students to many authors of fine literature in the hopes that each will find at least one who is appealing and interesting.

196 Students **write to living authors** to express pleasure at reading their books.

197 **Invite a local author** to talk to the class about his or her books and about the process of getting a book published.

198 **Compare the lives of authors** who have written similar types of books.

199 Help students experiment with **writing a story in the style of a favorite author.**

200 Arrange a **bulletin board display** of pictures, articles, book covers, and other materials about selected authors.

201 **Invite a librarian** to discuss children's authors.

202 Show **tapes, filmstrips, and videotapes** about the lives of selected authors.

203 Have the class read some **award-winning books.** Discuss why they were selected for distinction over other books.

204 Discuss the **difference between authors and author-illustrators.** Display examples of author-illustrator works. Discuss the special problems of author-illustrators.

205 Simulate an **interview or press conference** with an author.

206 Have each student **research a favorite author for an oral presentation.** Emphasize uniqueness and originality in the presentation and use of pictures and audiovisual aids. Students who are interested in art may choose to report on an author-illustrator.

Recommended Books about Authors and Writing

Aliki. *How a Book Is Made*. New York: Crowell, 1986.

Benjamin, Carol Lea. *Writing for Kids*. New York: Crowell, 1985.

Blair, Gwenda. *Laura Ingalls Wilder*. New York: Putnam, 1981.

Children's Book Council. *The Calendar*. (67 Irving Place, New York, NY, 10003)

Commire, Anne, ed. *Something About the Author* (multivolume reference). Detroit: Gale Research, 1971–.

De Montreville, Doris, and Donna Hill, eds. *Third Book of Junior Authors*. New York: Wilson, 1972.

Eaton, Jeanette. *America's Own Mark Twain*. New York: Morrow, 1958.

Franchere, Ruth. *Willa, The Story of Willa Cather's Growing Up*. New York: Crowell, 1958.

Fuller, Muriel, ed. *More Junior Authors*. New York: Wilson, 1969.

The Horn Book Magazine. Boston: Horn Book Inc.

Kunitz, Stanley J., and Howard Haycraft, eds. *The Junior Book of Authors,* 2d rev. ed. New York: Wilson, 1971.

Kyle, Elisabeth. *Girl with a Pen*. New York: Holt, Rinehart and Winston, 1966.

Meigs, Cornelia. *Invincible Louisa*. Boston: Little, Brown, 1933.

Quackenbush, Robert. *Mark Twain? What Kind of Name Is That?*

A Story of Samuel Langhorne Clemens. Englewood Cliffs: Prentice-Hall, 1984.

Spink, Reginald. *Hans Christian Andersen and His World.* New York: Putnam, 1972.

Taylor, Judy. *Beatrix Potter: Artist, Storyteller and Country Woman.* New York: Warne, 1986.

SPORTS

This theme usually takes little motivation since most students are interested in some sport, even if only as a spectator. It provides an opening for students to follow individual preferences and to share their pleasure with fellow classmates. Its development can include research and further reading related to a particular sport or personality. Such research may include newspaper articles, magazine stories, and information from other media, thus extending and broadening the learning experience. Consultation with a librarian will undoubtedly be needed to secure enough appropriate and worthwhile books to ensure the success of this theme.

207 Students **research the history of sports** in ancient Greece and Rome and other early cultures and note the significance of sports in each culture.

208 Students **research the history of a selected sport** and give an oral report to the class.

209 Arrange a **bulletin board display** of decorated book covers and student illustrations of scenes from sports stories interspersed with pictures of athletes and articles from magazines and newspapers.

210 Alone or as a group, students **invent and name an original game** complete with rules and a description of how to play it.

211 Periodically set aside time for sharing **brief oral book reviews** to familiarize the class with books that are available.

212 Create a **mural** of scenes from stories about sports. Try to depict as complete a picture as possible of sports in action. Include a variety of team and individual sports with not only famous athletes but also participants from several races and handicapped athletes. Draw the figures with chalk and then paint them with tempera. Outline the figures in black for a finishing touch. Each figure should be identified by name and book and briefly described to aid the viewers.

213 Divide the class into groups of students who have read the same book. Have each group create a **new ending for the story** they read. An interesting discussion can result from all the groups sharing their results.

214 Students compare **the ways different authors treat the same sport**. They should consider such factors as technical accuracy, relation to plot (incidental or major factors), and use as a vehicle for comedy.

215 Hold a **conversation between characters** from two different books about the same sport. The participants should read both books and be thoroughly familiar with the plots and characters. They should also plan questions they would like to ask and topics they would like to talk about.

216 Select a **newspaper article about a sports figure.** Analyze it to determine the difference between fact and inference.

217 Students research the **history of the Olympic Games.** Or they can research a selected Olympic sport (summer or winter). Have them share their reports for critique and discussion.

218 Students **write the rules for games played on the school grounds.** This project will require research and discussion with other students and staff.

219 Working alone or in groups, students **change the rules or organization of a popular game** and describe the adjustments needed—for example, adding a base to baseball (1st, 2nd, 3rd, 4th, and home).

220 **Invite an athlete** to talk to the class and describe the training and discipline of a specific sport. Students may prepare questions ahead of time to ensure a smooth presentation. During the talk students will take notes for a follow-up written summary of the important points made by the speaker.

Recommended Sports Books

Aaseng, Nathan. *Comeback Stars of Pro Sports*. Minneapolis: Lerner, 1983.
———. *Winners Never Quit: Athletes Who Beat the Odds*. Minneapolis: Lerner, 1980.
Anderson, Dave. *The Story of Football*. New York: Morrow, 1985.
Arnosky, Jim. *Flies in the Water, Fish in the Air*. New York: Lothrop, Lee & Shepard, 1986.
Ayer, Jacqueline. *NuDang and His Kite*. New York: Harcourt, Brace and World, 1959.
Bontemps, Arna. *Famous Negro Athletes*. New York: Dodd Mead, 1964.
Burchard, S. H. *Sports Star, Nadia Comaneci*. New York: Harcourt Brace Jovanovich, 1977.
Christopher, Matt. *The Team That Couldn't Lose*. Boston: Little Brown, 1967.
Cohen, Barbara. *Thank You, Jackie Robinson*. New York: Lothrop, Lee & Shepard, 1974.
Corbett, Scott. *The Hockey Girls*. New York: Dutton, 1976.
Fall, Thomas. *Jim Thorpe*. New York: Crowell, 1970.
Hahn, James, and Lynn Hahn. *The Career of Chris Evert Lloyd*. Mankato: Crestwood, 1981.
Hughes, Dean. *Nutty Can't Miss*. New York: Atheneum, 1987.
Jackson, Paul. *Uniform for Harry*. Chicago: Follett, 1962.
Kalb, Jonah, and Laura Kalb. *The Easy Skating Book*. Boston: Houghton Mifflin, 1981.
Krementz, Jill. *A Very Young Gymnast*. New York: Knopf, 1978.

Lipsyte, Robert. *The Contender*. New York: Bantam, 1969.

———. *Free to Be Muhammad Ali*. New York: Harper & Row, 1978.

Matsuno, Masako. *Chie and the Sports Day*. Cleveland: World, 1965.

Shortall, Leonard. *Ben on the Ski Trail*. New York: Morrow, 1965.

MEDIEVAL ADVENTURE STORIES

Because knights, castles, and tournaments seem to have a general appeal, it is usually easy to motivate students to read medieval adventure stories. To lovers of adventure and derring-do, this type of story is especially appealing. Carefully chosen books of this period can help students understand life in a bygone era and to appreciate that people have always had problems, many of which are similar to those we face today. This theme provides the opportunity to hone research skills in order to flesh out the historical background and explain medieval allusions.

221

Students **research** any of a number of interesting topics, such as
- the architecture and purpose of castles,
- how tournaments were conducted (with diagrams),
- dress (illustrated with drawings or paper dolls),
- different types of armor,
- early English history (including a diagram of the ruling houses and the line of ascension of British royalty),
- Anglo-Saxon versus Norman culture,
- the Crusades, and
- coat of arms emblems and figures.

222 As they read, students make **running charts** about how people lived, how they were governed, how they dressed, and so on. They can use these charts for reference for other projects.

223 Have students **design original castles** and accompany them with a description.

224 Students build **two dioramas:** one showing life in a castle and the other showing life in a village next to the castle. The dioramas should be labeled with an explanation for the viewers.

225 Groups **dramatize scenes** from several stories. Or they can dramatize a scene between a villager and a castle owner in which the villager presents the grievances of the vassals.

226 Each student **writes an original scene** set in a particular medieval place and time.

227 Students create **original family coats of arms** either for decoration or on a shield.

228 Arrange a **bulletin board display** of pictures of castles and life in medieval times. Add some original book jackets for favorite medieval adventure stories.

229 Make a **glossary of medieval words** and display it on a chart.

230 Hold a **conversation between two "castle owners,"** who discuss common problems with the government or the villagers or other topics such as mutual boundaries.

Recommended Medieval Adventure Books

Bennett, John. *Master Skylark*. New York: Airmont, [1896] 1924.
Buehr, Walter. *Knights and Castles*. New York: Putnam, 1975.
Bulla, Clyde. *The Sword in the Tree*. New York: Crowell, 1956.
Clarke, Anna. *The Queen of the Tournament*. Morristown: Silver, 1986.
de Angeli, Marguerite. *Black Fox of Lorne*. New York: Doubleday, 1957.

———. *The Door in the Wall*. New York: Doubleday, 1949.

Eager, Edward. *Knight's Castle*. New York: Harcourt Brace Jovanovich, 1985.

Fleischman, Sid. *The Whipping Boy*. New York: Greenwillow, 1986.

Kemp, Gene. *Jason Bodger and the Priory Ghost*. Winchester: Faber and Faber, 1985.

Lang, Andrew. *King Arthur: Tales of the Round Table*. New York: Scholastic, 1968.

Morris, Jean. *The Donkey's Crusade*. London: Bodley Head, 1983.

Rutland, Jonathan. *Knights and Castles*. New York: Random, 1987.

Scarry, Huck. *Looking into the Middle Ages*. New York: Harper & Row, 1984.

Siegel, Scott. *Revenge of the Falcon Knight*. New York: Avon, 1985.

Smith, E. K. *Black Tower*. New York: Vanguard, 1957.

Smythe, Malcolm, and Caroline Pitcher. *Build Your Own Castle*. New York: Franklin Watts, 1985.

Sutcliff, Rosemary. *The Light Beyond the Forest*. New York: Dutton, 1980.

———. *The Sword and the Circle*. New York: Dutton, 1981.

Tucker, Ernest. *The Story of Knights and Armor*. New York: Lothrop, Lee & Shepard, 1961.

Van Woerkom, Dorothy. *Pearl in the Egg*. New York: Crowell, 1980.

GREEK MYTHOLOGY

Since Greek mythology is the basis of much of our art and literature, our students should become familiar with it. The Greek word mythos, *which means tale or story, is the derivation of our word* myth. *Myths originated with early people as explanations for*

nature and natural phenomena. As time passed, heroic deeds of the gods and goddesses were incorporated, as were some historical events. The Greek myths are enjoyable tales that contain action, suspense, and conflict, the three major elements of a good story. Organize a display of books on Greek and Roman mythology, and be sure to include some of the fine anthologies.

Before they embark on any of the following activities, students should read a variety of books related to Greek mythology and discuss them and the relation of myths to the lives of the ancient Greeks. After studying Greek mythology, students may wish to explore the mythologies of other people—such as Japanese, Indian, and African.

231 As they read, students keep a **running chart of the gods and goddesses,** including their identity and their relationship to other deities.

232 Students research and chart **differences and similarities between Roman and Greek gods and goddesses.**

233 Create a **wall frieze** around the classroom depicting scenes from the lives of the gods and goddesses.

234 Each student writes an **original story about an incident in the life of a Greek mythical hero.**

235 Each student writes a **poem about an exciting mythological event.** For an effective presentation, the student can place the poem in the center of a 12-by-18-inch sheet of drawing paper and draw or paint illustrations around it.

236 Each student writes about an exciting event from mythology as a **"You Are There" report or the report of a news anchor.** Have the class share their reports aloud for discussion and enjoyment.

237 Students keep notebooks recording **examples of the influence of Greek mythology in our lives today,** such as Mars candy bars, Ajax cleaner, and Mercury automobiles. They can mount pictures, ads, wrappers, and package sides or tops on the pages with a description of the mythological origin of each name. A bulletin board display can be made of these examples as an alternative, but individual notebooks seem to generate more enthusiasm and more examples.

238 Use the class's creativity and imagination to create a **mural of the deities' home on Mount Olympus.**

239 Divide the class into two groups to **experiment with forms of dramatic presentation.** One group will write a play based on mythological incidents and then select a cast to read the play aloud. Meanwhile, the second group will select scenes, choose a cast, and prepare the play without writing the parts. Following both presentations, discuss the pros and cons of both methods.

240 Have students research the **sites in Greece and elsewhere where ruins related to the gods and goddesses can be found today,** such as Delos. Pinpoint the spots on a wall map. Complete the display with pictures, newspaper articles, and travel folders and magazines.

Recommended Books of Greek Mythology

Alexander, Beatrice. *Famous Myths of the Golden Age.* New York: Random, 1947.

Benson, Sally. *Stories of the Gods and Heroes.* New York: Dial, 1940.

Bulfinch, Thomas. *Age of Fable.* New York: Macmillan, 1942.

D'Aulaire, Ingri, and Edgar D'Aulaire. *D'Aulaires' Book of Greek Myths.* New York: Doubleday, 1962.

Evslin, Barnard, and Dorothy Evslin. *The Greek Gods.* New York: Scholastic, 1984.

Gates, Doris. *The Golden God: Apollo.* New York: Penguin, 1983.

———. *Two Queens of Heaven: Aphrodite and Demeter.* New York: Penguin, 1983.

———. *The Warrior Goddess: Athena.* New York: Penguin, 1972.

Low, Alice. *The Macmillan Book of Greek Gods and Heroes.* New York: Macmillan, 1985.

Naden, C. J. *Jason and the Golden Fleece.* New York: Troll, 1980.

———. *Pegasus, the Winged Horse.* New York: Troll, 1980.

Storr, Catherine. *King Midas.* Milwaukee: Raintree, 1985.

———. *Theseus and the Minotaur.* Milwaukee: Raintree, 1986.

Weil, Lisl. *Pandora's Box.* New York: Macmillan, 1986.

FAMILIES

The family today takes many forms. Many books are available depicting a wide variety of family situations and relationships and realistically describing the inherent problems and the vicissitudes that family members face. Some students reading such stories can identify with the characters as they work toward solving their problems; others can gain understanding of family members in circumstances different from their own; and still others may learn appreciation for their personal situations. Make an eclectic collection of books available, one that has stories about many diverse family groups and situations. Here's where a librarian can really help.

241 Create a **bulletin board display** of drawings or cut-outs of book families. Label each family and note the book in which it appears.

242 Have a group of students who have read the same book **assume the roles of family members** and discuss family relationships and how they solved their problems. The group should prepare by reviewing the book and planning the topics for discussion. Classmates who are not participating in the discussion can contribute ideas too.

243 Students construct **mobiles** of members of a family and special objects in their lives.

244 Conduct a **TV interview or a panel discussion** in which several characters from different books discuss their relationships with their parents and siblings. Several groups may prepare interviews with different characters. Everyone taking part should have read all the books from which the characters come.

245 Each student writes a **comparison of how two characters from different books handled a similar problem or situation.** Students can read papers aloud to stimulate discussion.

246 Encourage students to **discuss personal experiences that are similar to situations in the books** they have read. Have them compare their solutions to the ones in the books.

247 As a class project or individually, students **write a play** about a mythical family and its adventures. If this is done as a class project, have the students read or perform the play.

Recommended Books about Families

Alexander, Martha. *Nobody Asked Me If I Wanted a Baby Sister*. New York: Dial, 1971.

Blume, Judy. *It's Not the End of the World*. New York: Bradbury, 1972.

Byars, Betsy. *The Summer of the Swans*. New York: Viking, 1970.

Carlson, Natalie. *The Family Under the Bridge*. New York: Harper & Row, 1958.

Dalgleish, Alice. *The Courage of Sarah Noble*. New York: Macmillan, 1954.

Estes, Eleanor. *The Moffats*. New York: Harcourt, Brace and World, 1941.

Greene, Betty. *Them That Glitter and Them That Don't*. New York: Knopf, 1983.

Guilfoil, Elizabeth. *Nobody Listens to Andrew*. Chicago: Follett, 1957.

Johnson, Annabel, and Edgar Johnson. *The Grizzly*. New York: Harper & Row, 1964.

Kenkes, Kevin. *Two Under Par*. New York: Scholastic, 1987.

MacLachlan, Patricia. *Sarah, Plain and Tall*. New York: Harper & Row, 1985.

Mark, Jan. *Trouble Half-Way*. New York: Atheneum, 1986.

Neville, Emily. *It's Like This, Cat*. New York: Harper & Row, 1963.

Ryan, Mary C. *Frankie's Run*. Boston: Little, Brown, 1987.

Shotwell, Louisa. *Roosevelt Grady*. New York: Philomel, 1963.

Snyder, Zilpha K. *The Birds of Summer*. New York: Atheneum, 1983.

Sonneborn, Ruth. *Friday Night Is Papa's Night*. New York: Penguin, 1987.

Stevenson, James. *Will You Please Feed Our Cat?* New York: Greenwillow, 1987.

Taylor, Sydney. *All-of-a-Kind Family*. Chicago: Follett, 1951.

Wilder, Laura Ingalls. *Little House on the Prairie*. New York: Harper & Row, 1953.

FRIENDSHIP

Friendships are important to all boys and girls, so they readily identify with book characters in this type of story. They can understand their problems and changes in relationships, but of most interest is how the book characters solve their problems. Students who feel they have no friends will learn they are not unique as they read about others who feel the same way but work out a satisfactory solution. Students' insight and understanding will grow as they read stories about friendships that cross such barriers as age, race, color, or social standing. Their values, too, may be influenced as they read stories that emphasize such attributes as loyalty, honesty, and trust. Before attempting any of the activities, students should read and discuss many books to develop a background from which they can draw as they participate in the activities.

248

Hold a **panel discussion** about the various kinds of friendships found in the books that students have read. Another panel could discuss how friendship affected the lives of the characters and what might have happened had the friendship not existed. Or "interview" the characters about what they think might have happened to them if they had not met their friends.

249 Have students **document examples of friendship** in newspaper and magazine articles and on television.

250 Students **create stories or poems** about a friendship or friendships.

251 **Play tapes and show movies** of stories depicting special friendships. You'll find a number of them in your audiovisual department.

252 Use a variety of media—paint, cut paper, crayon—for a **display of storybook friendships.** Don't forget to label each one.

253 Have students present **oral book reports of stories about warm friendships.** Remind them to summarize the plot, omit unnecessary details, and include an objective critique.

254 Each student **writes an original story**—autobiographical or fictional—that has friendship as its theme.

255 Have each student **write and illustrate a poem** about friendship or a special friendship. Gather the poems for a classroom display.

256 Create a painted or cut-paper **wall frieze** of important moments of several storybook friendships. Include a brief explanation under each picture noting the book and the friendship depicted.

Recommended Books about Friendship

Aaron, Chester. *An American Ghost*. New York: Harcourt Brace Jovanovich, 1973.

Anglund, Joan Walsh. *A Friend Is Someone Who Likes You*. New York: Harcourt Brace Jovanovich, 1958.

Byars, Betsy. *Cracker Jackson*. New York: Viking, 1985.

Cassedy, Sylvia. *M. E. and Morton*. New York: Crowell, 1987.

Cunningham, Julia. *Burnish Me Bright*. New York: Pantheon, 1970.

Graeber, Charlotte. *Grey Cloud*. Bristol: Four Winds, 1979.

Greene, Constance C. *A Girl Called Al*. New York: Viking, 1969.

Griffith, Helen. *The Greyhound*. New York: Harcourt Brace Jovanovich, 1973.

Grund, Josef Carl. *You Have a Friend, Pietro*. Boston: Little, Brown, 1966.

Hansen, Joyce. *A Yellow Bird and Me*. New York: Clarion, 1986.

Hoff, Syd. *Who Will Be My Friends?* New York: Harper & Row, 1960.

Howard, Ellen. *Edith Herself*. New York: Atheneum, 1987.

Krumgold, Joseph. *Onion John*. New York: Crowell, 1959.

Lobel, Arnold. *Frog and Toad Are Friends*. New York: Harper & Row, 1970.

Mayne, William. *Drift*. New York: Delacorte, 1986.

Rosenberg, Maxine. *My Friend Leslie: The Story of a Handicapped Child*. New York: Lothrop, Lee & Shepard, 1983.

Sachs, Muriel. *Underdog*. New York: Doubleday, 1985.

Simon, Shirley. *Best Friend*. Lothrop, Lee & Shepard, 1964.

Speare, Elizabeth George. *The Sign of the Beaver*. Boston: Houghton Mifflin, 1983.

Udry, Janice May. *Let's Be Enemies*. New York: Harper & Row, 1961.

MYSTERIES

Suspense, secrets, the unknown, and spies are all elements that arouse the student's interest, so this theme is easy to initiate. The library bookshelves offer all kinds of mysteries: ones that involve children or young people as detectives, ones built around a mysterious person, ones that involve a secret, ones about a treasure, science fiction mysteries, and historical mysteries. Make available a collection of different types of mysteries to encourage students to read more than one type. Many mysteries for young people are

written as a series about the same character, but since all the books in a series usually have similar plot structures, it is wise to suggest that students read only one book per series for a mystery unit.

A carefully selected mystery read aloud can make a special contribution to this theme's activities.

257 Have a **class discussion** about the various types of mysteries, the patterns followed by some mystery writers, and the techniques writers use to maintain the reader's interest. For example, some books reveal the mystery's solution at the beginning and then the story shows how the mystery was solved. Some mysteries have a single plot line, and others have several subplots that all come together in the end. Some authors only hint at the mystery in the beginning, and others lay out the plot in the first paragraph.

258 Create a bulletin board **display of student-designed and -decorated book covers** for mystery books. Each cover should include a brief blurb on the front flap to entice the reader, and a paragraph or two about the author on the back flap.

259 Stage a **"meeting" of several fictional sleuths** discussing their cases. To have an effective discussion, students who assume the roles will need to be very familiar not only with their character and book but also with the books about every sleuth selected.

260 Have each student **write an original mystery** story. They read their stories *except for the endings* aloud to classmates. Let the group discuss possible solutions before the author reveals the intended ending.

Or each student can **recount a mystery story (except for the ending)** that he or she has read, and let the audience compare solutions with the author's. Remind students to describe only the main points of the plot that are germane to solving the mystery and to avoid unnecessary details.

261 Each student constructs a **picto-map** showing the steps a fictional character took to solve a mystery. First, they draw a large map of the locale of the story. Then they indicate, with an appropriate picture or design and a brief explanatory label, each step taken to reach the solution.

262 **Invite a local mystery author** to visit the class to discuss the writing of a mystery. Be sure to have a display of the author's books. Perhaps he or she would like to hear some of the mysteries written by students.

263 Students construct **dioramas** depicting a key scene from a mystery story.

264 Students construct **roller movies** retelling a favorite mystery story. Have them stop the action and narration before the mystery is solved so that the audience can guess the ending. This activity is especially effective if the story is one that has been read only by the group of students making the roller movie.

Recommended Mysteries

Adler, David A. *Cam Jansen and the Mystery of the Stolen Diamonds*. New York: Viking, 1980.

Alexander, Lloyd. *The El Dorado Adventure*. New York: Dutton, 1987.

Ancharsvard, Karin. *Madcap Mystery*. New York: Harcourt, Brace and World, 1962.

Anderson, Mary. *Matilda Investigates*. New York: Atheneum, 1973.

Babbitt, Natalie. *The Eyes of the Amaryllis*. New York: Farrar, Straus and Giroux, 1977.

Bonham, Roy. *Mystery of the Fat Cat*. New York: Dell, 1971.

Corbin, William. *A Dog Worth Stealing*. New York: Orchard/Watts, 1987.

Corcoran, Barbara. *Mystery on Ice*. New York: Atheneum, 1985.

Fitzhugh, Louise. *Harriet the Spy*. New York: Harper & Row, 1964.

Freeman, Gail. *Alien Thunder*. New York: Bradbury, 1982.

Gunning, Thomas G. *Strange Mysteries*. New York: Dodd, 1987.

Hamilton, Virginia. *The Mystery of Drear House*. New York: Greenwillow, 1987.

Hildick, E. W. *Manhattan Is Missing*. New York: Avon, 1983.

Park, Ruth. *Playing Beatie Bow*. New York: Argo/Atheneum, 1982.

Pearce, Philippa. *Who's Afraid? And Other Strange Stories*. New York: Greenwillow, 1986.

Quackenbush, Robert. *Stage Door to Terror*. New York: Prentice-Hall, 1984.

Shreve, Susan. *Lucy Forever and Mrs. Rosetree, Shrinks.* New York: Knopf, 1988.

Singer, Marilyn. *The Case of the Crackling Car.* New York: Harper & Row, 1985.

———. *A Clue in Code.* New York: Harper & Row, 1985.

Snyder, Zilpha K. *The Velvet Room.* New York: Atheneum, 1965.

Taylor, Mark. *The Case of the Purloined Compass.* New York: Atheneum, 1985.

HISTORICAL FICTION

One of the most effective ways to interest students in history is through the medium of historical fiction. Good historical fiction can give readers a feeling for life during the period depicted. They learn the hardships and difficulties people living in earlier times had to overcome. Stories based on historical facts help students understand today in terms of what happened yesterday. Important, too, in motivating students to read is that historical fiction usually contains much action and suspense and in general is a "good read." Wide reading and discussion will lay a solid groundwork for the activities.

265 Create a **bulletin board display of student-decorated book covers** interspersed with pictures of historical scenes and events described in the books. Students collect pictures from magazines or other sources or paint them.

266 Each student selects a particularly exciting or interesting event in a book and writes it in the form of an **entry in the diary of the main character** of the book.

267 Mount a large **map of the world.** As students read, they pin a flag with the title and the author on the locale of the book. Allot several opportunities each week for students to briefly share the books they have added to the map.

268 To establish a sense of time, the class constructs a **time line** (divided into centuries) and enters the title of each book read in the appropriate column.

269 Have the students each assume the role of someone living in the same era (perhaps a character from another book) and **write a letter** to a selected book character.

270 Each student **writes about an episode** in the life of a major character as seen through the eyes of a lesser character in the same book.

271 Hold a **panel discussion** among students who have read several books about different eras of American history. They can discuss and compare the country and the way that people lived in the different eras.
  Or you can stage a **discussion among characters** from several books set in the same period. If desired, participants can dress in appropriate costumes. For either activity, students should prepare the points they wish to make, although others will undoubtedly arise during the discussion.

272 Students who have read the same book **dramatize selected scenes** from the book. The dramatization can be simple with quickly improvised props or an elaborate costumed performance. The goal is interpretation and characterization.

273 Each student **pretends to be an illustrator** who has been hired to make three illustrations for a selected book. This task requires deciding which three scenes to illustrate and which media is most appropriate. After the illustrations are completed, have each artist explain his or her choices.

274

As a class or individual activity, students **write new lyrics for a popular folk tune** such as "Skip to My Lou" to tell about an event or a character in one of the books they have read.

Recommended Historical Fiction

Brenner, Barbara. *Wagon Wheels*. New York: Harper & Row, 1978.

Brink, Carol Ryrie. *Caddie Woodlawn*. New York: Macmillan, 1935.

Bulla, Clyde. *Ride the Pony Express*. New York: Crowell, 1954.

Crow, Donna E. *Professor 2's Mysterious Machine*. Elgin: Cook, 1983.

Dalgliesh, Alice. *The Courage of Sarah Noble*. New York: Macmillan, 1986.

de Angeli, Marguerite. *The Door in the Wall*. New York: Doubleday, 1949.

DeJong, Meindert. *House of Sixty Fathers*. New York: Harper & Row, 1956.

Forbes, Esther. *Johnnie Tremain*. Boston: Houghton Mifflin, 1943.

Fritz, Jean. *And Then What Happened, Paul Revere?* New York: Putnam, 1973.

Gray, Elizabeth J. *Adam of the Road*. New York: Viking, 1942.

Greene, Bette. *Summer of My German Soldier*. New York: Dial, 1973.

Haugaard, Eric. *Hakon of Rogen's Saga*. Boston: Houghton Mifflin, 1965.

Hirschfelder, Arlene. *Happily May I Walk*. New York: Macmillan, 1986.

Longfellow, Henry Wadsworth. *Paul Revere's Ride*. New York: Greenwillow, 1985.

MacLachlan, Patricia. *Sarah, Plain and Tall*. New York: Harper & Row, 1985.

McSwigan, Marie. *Snow Treasure*. New York: Dutton, 1964.

Monjo, F. N. *The Drinking Gourd*. New York: Harper & Row, 1970.

O'Dell, Scott. *The King's Fifth*. Boston: Houghton Mifflin, 1966.

——. *Sing Down the Moon*. Boston: Houghton Mifflin, 1970.

Petry, Ann. *Harriet Tubman: Conductor on the Underground Railroad*. New York: Crowell, 1955.

Saiki, Patsy Sumie. *Saiki: A Daughter of Hawaii*. Tokyo: Kisaki, 1977.

Speare, Elizabeth George. *The Sign of the Beaver*. Boston: Houghton Mifflin, 1983.

Taylor, Theodore. *The Cay*. New York: Avon, 1977.

Uchida, Yoshiko. *Journey to Topaz*. New York: Harper & Row, 1975.

LONELINESS

Many students can readily identify with this theme, since loneliness can strike anywhere—in a classroom or in an empty house. Students may learn the difference between being alone and being lonely as they read about people who have been alone but not lonely because they had inner resources on which to draw. They will read how characters who suffered loneliness for long periods of time combatted it. They may learn the need for periods of quiet and solitude in this busy world in order to be creative and to achieve certain goals. As students read about how characters who are lonely or alone coped with their situations, they may grow in insight and self-understanding. Before beginning the activities, much reading and discussion should take place.

275 Encourage a **discussion comparing the types of loneliness** found in different books and the ways that each character coped with it.

276 Have each student **compose a poem** about loneliness.

277 Have each student **create a picture** that expresses loneliness.

278 Have each student **write an essay** describing a time when they felt lonely.

279 Students **read aloud selected paragraphs** that they feel best describe loneliness in the book they have read.

280 From a favorite book, each student makes a **list of the words and phrases that describe loneliness.**

281 Each student assumes the role of the leading character of a book and writes **diary entries** recording a traumatic event in the character's life.

282 Students portraying **characters from several books discuss and compare their experiences**. Participants in this discussion should have read all the books because familiarity with the lives and backgrounds of all the characters will help the discussion flow smoothly and thoughtfully.

283 Students work in groups to construct **dioramas** depicting crucial scenes in several books. Encourage them to select colors and materials (papier-mâché, paint, twigs, rocks, and other small objects) that will impart a feeling of loneliness. Each diorama should be labeled with the book's title and author and a brief description of the scene.

Recommended Books about Loneliness

Byars, Betsy. *The Summer of the Swans*. New York: Viking, 1970.

Caudill, Rebecca. *The Far-Off Land*. New York: Viking, 1964.

DeJong, Meindert. *The Singing Hill*. New York: Harper & Row, 1962.

Estes, Esther. *The Hundred Dresses*. New York: Harcourt, Brace and World, 1944.

George, Jean. *Julie of the Wolves*. New York: Harper & Row, 1972.

———. *My Side of the Mountain*. New York: Dutton, 1959.

Henry, Marguerite. *King of the Wind*. New York: Macmillan, 1948.

Johnson, Doris. *Su An*. Chicago: Follett, 1968.

Konigsburg, E. L. *Jennifer, Hecate, Macbeth, William McKinley, and Me, Elizabeth*. New York: Atheneum, 1967.

Kroeber, Theodora. *Ishi, Last of His Tribe*. Boston: Houghton Mifflin, 1964.

Krumgold, Joseph. *Onion John*. New York: Crowell, 1959.

O'Dell, Scott. *Island of the Blue Dolphins*. Boston: Houghton Mifflin, 1960.

Ottley, Reginald. *Boy Alone*. New York: Harcourt Brace Jovanovich, 1965.

Paterson, Katherine. *The Great Gilly Hopkins*. New York: Crowell, 1978.

Richter, Conrad. *The Light in the Forest*. New York: Bantam, 1963.

Sperry, Armstrong. *Call It Courage*. New York: Macmillan, 1940.

Treffinger, Carolyn. *Li Lun, Lad of Courage*. Nashville: Abington, 1947.

Weik, Mary Hays. *Jazz Man*. New York: Atheneum, 1966.

Weiner, Sandra. *It's Wings That Make Birds Fly, The Story of a Boy*. New York: Pantheon, 1968.

Weir, Esther. *The Loner*. New York: McKay, 1963.

Yoshima, Taro. *Crow Boy*. New York: Viking, 1955.

ANIMALS

Stories about animals have a natural appeal for students, so this theme usually becomes one that generates its own enthusiasm. Small children can identify emotionally with an animal who is small and dependent on others, and all young readers admire such traits found in animals as intelligence, loyalty, courage, and the ability to give love. Horses are usually a particular favorite with the girls. Boys as a rule like any good animal story, especially one with lots of action. Many animal stories portray change not only on the part of the animal but in the human character as well, as a result of the growing relationship between human and animal. To help students develop deeper understanding and sensitivity, encourage them to read books about different animals rather than concentrating on books about their favorite ones.

284 Display a student collection of **model and toy animals.** Use a bulletin board filled with pictures, articles, and student-decorated book covers as a backdrop.

285 Each student compiles a **notebook of animal pictures.** Use 12-by-18-inch construction paper. Punch two or three holes in the sheets and tie them together with yarn. The pictures can be drawn or cut out of magazines. Each animal's name should be written under its picture and, if desired, a description of the animal and its habits.

286 Take the class on a study **trip to the zoo** to see the animals they have met in books.

287 Each student writes an **original story about an animal** selected from the classroom display (No. 284), one seen at the zoo (No. 286), or a favorite pet. The student can then share it with others for discussion and comments.

288 Each student writes and illustrates a **poem about one or more animals.** After they have printed or written the poem on a large piece of paper and decorated it, add it to the classroom display (No. 284).

289 Students make two-column **charts to compare two books about the same animal.** Comparisons can be made of the appearance and behavior of the animals.

290 Set aside a time for students to **share their own experiences** with their pets or other animals.

291 Stage a **conversation between two book characters** who have had experiences with animals, such as Julie (*Julie of the Wolves*) and Karana (*Island of the Blue Dolphins*).

292 Students **dramatize scenes** from some of the stories. An interesting technique for younger children is to use name signs for the characters and scenery. Children hold signs and assume appropriate positions for the characters or objects (such as tables, trees, or rocks) they represent. The dialogue can be spontaneous or read by a narrator.

Recommended Books about Animals

Angelo, Valenti. *The Tale of a Donkey*. New York: Viking, 1966.

Barrett, Judi. *Animals Should Definitely Not Act Like People*. New York: Atheneum, 1980.

Brett, Jan. *Annie and the Wild Animals*. Boston: Houghton Mifflin, 1985.

Burnford, Sheila. *The Incredible Journey*. Boston: Little, Brown, 1961.

Byars, Betsy. *The Midnight Fox*. New York: Viking, 1968.

Carris, Joan. *Pets, Vets and Marty Howard*. New York: Harper & Row, 1984.

Carter, Anne. *Bella's Secret Garden*. New York: Crown, 1987.

Dalgliesh, Alice. *Bears on Hemlock Mountain*. New York: Scribners, 1952.

Farley, Walter. *Black Stallion*. New York: Random House, 1941.

Fox, Paula. *One-eyed Cat*. New York: Bradbury, 1984.

George, Jean. *Julie of the Wolves*. New York: Harper & Row, 1972.

Gipson, Fred. *Old Yeller*. New York: Harper, 1956.

Goble, Paul. *The Girl Who Loved Wild Horses*. New York: Bradbury, 1978.

Henry, Marguerite. *Brighty of Grand Canyon*. Skokie: Rand McNally, 1953.

———. *King of the Wind*. New York: Macmillan, 1948.

———. *Misty of Chincoteague*. Skokie: Rand McNally, 1947.

Holmes, E. T. *Amy's Goose*. New York: Harper & Row, 1977.

Jarrell, Randall. *Animal Family*. New York: Pantheon, 1965.

King-Smith, Dick. *Babe: The Gallant Pig*. New York: Crown, 1983.

Kjelgaard, Jim. *Big Red*. New York: Holiday House, 1956.

Morey, Walt. *Gentle Ben*. New York: Dutton, 1965.

O'Dell, Scott. *Island of the Blue Dolphins*. Boston: Houghton Mifflin, 1960.

Steig, William. *Abel's Island*. New York: Farrar, Straus and Giroux, 1976.

Ward, Lynd. *The Biggest Bear*. Boston: Houghton Mifflin, 1952.

Weaver, Harriet E. *Frosty: A Raccoon to Remember*. New York: Archway, 1977.

QUESTIONS TO STIMULATE BOOK DISCUSSIONS

Because most of the activities in this book grow out of discussion, here are a few suggestions for questions to stimulate thinking and to motivate interaction. You undoubtedly will have more.

Character
- How did the characters face difficulty?
- What were their relationships with others?
- What were their strongest characteristics?
- Which character did you think was strongest? Why? Which one did you think was weakest? Why?
- Compare the characters in books about the same theme (such as loneliness, growing up, large families, a new baby). How are the characters alike? How are they different?
- How do you think the characters from different books would have acted if they had met? Do you think they would have gotten along well? Explain your answer.
- How would the characters in a given book have responded to the situation in another book? Would they respond in the same way as that book's characters did? Explain why or why not.

Plot
- How did the author sustain the reader's interest?
- How did the author build the story to a climax?
- How did the author create an atmosphere for the story?

Style
- How did the author build the characters?
- How did the author use dialogue to describe a character? Read an example.
- Why was one book more interesting, more exciting, sadder, or harder or easier to read than another? Give examples.
- After having read several books by the same author, do you notice any typical characteristics or patterns in the stories? Describe them.

SUGGESTIONS FOR SUCCESSFUL GROUP WORK

Group work can be enjoyable for both the students and the teacher if a few simple guidelines are followed. These guidelines are based on wide experience in conducting group work at all grade levels and with many types of students.

1. Plan! Think through what you expect to accomplish with this group work and how you expect to accomplish it.

   Stop to reflect for a few moments on your objectives for group work. They might include learning to develop initiative, to assume responsibility, to share ideas, to respect the talents of others, to develop leadership abilities, to work independently, and simply how to work in a group. In the process of attaining these objectives, students will gain knowledge in a broad spectrum of subject areas and skills.

2. Divide the class into groups of a workable size (usually not more than five, and three works best). Because the students should select the project on which they will work, the size of the groups may vary.

   Pay attention to the composition of the groups: as the teacher, you know that to assure maximum learning, certain students should not work together. In this case a simple "Jack, today Bill's group needs you to work with them" is usually effective if said casually and with a certain amount of firmness.

3. Appoint a leader for each group. Again, do it casually. This is not being dictatorial; it is part of your direction of and involvement in the activity. Select someone you know is reliable and will see that the group works to complete its project. The leader can also have the responsibility of stopping work at the agreed-upon time for clean-up and of seeing that all is left in order.

   The leader is your liaison with each group when you need to check on plans or progress or when the group needs to communicate with you.

   Playing the role of group leader is good leadership training, which is an important objective of work in groups.

4. Once the members of each group have decided on their project, they should prepare a sketch or outline of what they plan to do.

This is the time for you to evaluate the scope of their plans. Are they realistic? Is the project too easy or too complex? Are the necessary materials available? Can it be completed in the allotted time? Help the group to adjust its plans, if necessary. This will assure an orderly procedure and avoid confusion and delay when the work period begins.

5. At the beginning of the work period, check with the leader of each group to be sure that all know what they are going to do and that the needed materials are on hand.

It's a good idea to remind the leaders to check on each member of their group individually. These are the kinds of details that can make or break an activity period!

6. Once the work period has begun, the noise level will rise. When it gets too loud, call for a minute of silence, and then begin work again with a reminder that it is necessary to use soft voices when so many people are working.

7. Decide on a quitting time before the work begins to allow time for clean-up, evaluation of work accomplished, and planning the project's next steps.

8. Make sure that every project is completed unless an unavoidable situation prevents it. An unfinished project usually indicates it was begun with no real object in mind.

9. Have material ready for an alternative activity in the event that one group cannot work on its activity on a particular day or that it finishes ahead of the others. An art activity is usually a good choice—for example, creating a picture related to the theme with paints, crayons, or cut paper, or cutting out and mounting as a collage pictures or parts of pictures related to the theme or to a story. Whatever the alternative activity, it should be related to the theme and it should be one that was previously demonstrated to keep disruption of the work session minimal.

BIBLIOGRAPHY

Adams, Bess Porter. *About Books and Children*. New York: Holt, 1953.

Anderson, Paul S. *Storytelling with the Flannel Board, Book One*. Minneapolis: Dennison, 1963.

Anderson, Verna Dieckman. *Reading and Young Children*. New York: Macmillan, 1968.

Applegate, Maureen. *Easy in English*. New York: Harper & Row, 1964.

Arbuthnot, May Hill. *The Arbuthnot Anthology of Children's Literature*. rev. ed. Chicago: Scott, Foresman, 1961.

———. *Children and Books*. 3d ed. Chicago: Scott, Foresman, 1968.

———. *Time for Fairy Tales*. Chicago: Scott, Foresman, 1961.

———. *Time for Poetry*. Chicago: Scott, Foresman, 1968.

Carlson, Ruth Kearney. *Enrichment Ideas*. 2d ed. Dubuque: Brown, 1976.

Chambers, Dewey. *Children's Literature in the Curriculum*. Chicago: Rand McNally: 1971.

———. *Literature for Children: Storytelling and Creative Drama*. Dubuque: Brown, 1970.

Cianciolo, Patricia. *Literature for Children: Illustrations in Children's Books*. Dubuque: Brown, 1966.

Cullinan, Bernice E., ed. *Children's Literature in the Reading Program*. Newark, DE: International Reading Association, 1987.

Dallman, Martha. *Teaching the Language Arts in the Elementary School*. Dubuque: Brown, 1966.

Early, Margaret, ed. *Wider Than the Sky*. New York: Harcourt, Brace and World, 1968.

George, Mary Yanaga. *Language Art, An Idea Book*. Scranton: Chandler, 1970.

Georgiou, Constantine. *Children and Their Literature*. Englewood Cliffs, NJ: Prentice-Hall, 1969.

Glazer, Joan I. *Literature for Young Children*. Columbus: Merrill, 1986.

Hazard, Paul. *Books, Children and Men*. Translated by Margaret Mitchell. Boston: The Horn Book, 1947.

Hickler, Holly, and C. Lowell May. *Creative Writing: From Thought to Action*. Boston: Allyn and Bacon, 1979.

Huck, Charlotte S., and Doris Young Kuhn. *Children's Literature in the Elementary School*. 2d ed. New York: Holt, Rinehart and Winston, 1968.

Johnson, Edna, Evelyn R. Sickles, and Frances Clarke Sayers. *Anthology of Children's Literature*. 5th ed. Boston: Houghton Mifflin, 1977.

Kaplan, Sandra, et al. *Change for Children*. Pacific Palisades: Goodyear, 1973.

Nebraska Curriculum Center. *A Curriculum for English*. Lincoln: University of Nebraska Press, 1966.

Norton, Donna. *Through the Eyes of a Child: An Introduction to Children's Literature*. Columbus: Merrill, 1983.

Painter, Helen W. *Reaching Children and Young People Through Literature*. Newark: DE: International Reading Association, 1971.

Petty, Walter T., and Mary E. Bowen. *Slithery Snakes and Other Aids to Children's Writing*. New York: Appleton-Century-Crofts, 1967.

Sawyer, Ruth. *The Way of the Storyteller*. rev. ed. New York: Viking, 1962.

Shapiro, Jon E., ed. *Using Literature and Poetry Effectively*. Newark, DE: International Reading Association, 1979.

Smith, James A. *Creative Teaching of Reading and Literature in the Elementary School*. Boston: Allyn and Bacon, 1967.

Sutherland, Zena, and Myra Livingston. *The Scott, Foresman Anthology of Children's Literature*. Glenview: Scott, Foresman, 1984.

About the Author

Dr. Geiger graduated from Lowell University in Massachusetts with a bachelor's degree in education. After teaching for several years, she migrated to California where she earned a master's degree at San Francisco State University and a doctorate from the University of California, Berkeley. She began her teaching career in Vermont in a one-room school with 27 children in six grades. Since then she has taught every grade from 1 through 8 plus classes in dramatics, art, and music in Massachusetts and California. She has also been an elementary and intermediate school administrator, a curriculum consultant for grades K–12, and a professor of education at Sonoma State University, where she has been honored with the title Emeritus. She has also served as a member of the board of directors of the California Reading Association and as editor of the *California Reader*.